Family Grouping in the Primary School

Family Grouping in the Primary School

BY LORNA RIDGWAY   *Senior Lecturer*
in Education
Stockwell College
of Education

AND IRENE LAWTON   *Headmistress*
Manford CP
Infants' School

WARD LOCK EDUCATIONAL

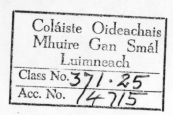
7062 3045 0 Hardback
7062 3293 3 Paperback
First published 1965
Reprinted 1967
Second edition completely revised and enlarged 1968
Reprinted 1969
Reprinted 1973

Originally published as *Family Grouping in the Infants' School*

Set in Monotype Times New Roman 10 on 11 point

Printed in Great Britain by
Redwood Press Limited
Trowbridge, Wiltshire

Contents

	Introduction	7
	Preface	9
	Preface to the second edition	12
1	Family Grouping: What is it? Why do it?	13
2	Aims and Purposes: Ways and Means	23
3	Emotional Development	40
4	Social Development	64
5	Intellectual Development	75
6	Class Lessons	112
7	The Teacher	130
8	Ways of Using Family Grouping	140
9	Changing the Traditional Pattern	149
10	A Variety of Views	156
11	Vertical Classification in the Junior (Middle) School	169
	Bibliography	181
	Index	186

Introduction

For many years my work was to visit the elementary schools of a large city. Then I was moved to a rural area, and most of my time was spent visiting the schools in small and often remote villages. It is easy to be sentimental about the village school; but I found that, as in the town, a few were good, some were bad, and most were somewhere in between. In the village school however when it *was* good there was a quality I had never found before; in their resourcefulness, in their mutual understanding, in their whole bearing, the children showed a maturity of growth that even the best town schools lacked. Later my work took me on visits throughout England and I had an opportunity not only of confirming the experience I have described, but of posing in a wide variety of circumstances a question which demanded an answer: what was it that gave this quality peculiar to the good village school?

The circumstances and conditions of a village school differ in many respects from those of a town school. Perhaps the most striking is the difference in their size. The town school is usually large, with many classes, often two or three classes for each year of school life. The village school has only one, or two, or occasionally three classes altogether, and in these are taught children ranging in age from 5 to 11 years. In such classes there is inevitably a wide age range, and the best way to make a virtue of necessity is to try to encourage the children to help each other, and so to make learning a cooperative rather than a competitive activity. I was beginning to suspect that it was their success in this way of learning which gave the peculiar quality to a good village school when I visited in a small town an Infants' school whose children were arranged in a novel manner. There were seven classes to cover the two and a bit years which for most children is their Infants' school life; but each class included the whole age range from 5 to 7 plus years—that is to say the school was arranged in seven

7

parallel classes. It was a good school by any standard; but here, and for the first time in a larger school, I experienced that peculiar quality of a good village school: the children had a resourcefulness, a mutual understanding, and a bearing that marked an unusual maturity of growth.

This happened quite a long time ago; and since then many other Infants' teachers have adopted a similar arrangement of their children, and call it 'Family Grouping'. No doubt their journey to this destination was less circuitous and faltering than mine: it is traditional for Infants' teachers quickly to recognize a good thing when they see it and to make it theirs. But the surprising thing is how relatively few teachers have seen this arrangement in action; and until it has been experienced the quality it can give to the children's learning is not easy to imagine. On the other hand the difficulties which might face the teachers in a Family-grouped school are easy to imagine, and only experience can convince how much less formidable these really are than is thought. This book sets out in detail what happens in an Infants' school with Family Grouping; it describes the problems and how these can usually be forestalled or solved; and it quotes the observations of many teachers who have had experience of teaching in this way.

It is indeed a way of teaching, or rather a way of learning. Education is about people, especially young people; and one of the most remarkable characteristics of people young and old is how few live using their powers to the full. Most of us are able to use no more than a fraction of our potential. We shall not release these undeveloped powers by teaching children to read at two years old: that merely attempts to induce precocity with its attendant ills. Young children grow to the full when they live in an environment which encourages growth. Material things are an important part of this environment. The most important part is the climate of thought and feeling created by those adults in whose care the children are. It is a climate which gives guidance and at the same time opportunity for choice, in which learning does not mean beating your neighbour or gaining ticks, but is a cooperative venture of all concerned. Such a climate can be created only by human thought and feeling; but I know of no arrangement of a school which helps so much to this end as does Family Grouping.

This book comes from the experience of sensitive and successful teaching. It will rouse interest in those who have no experience of Family Grouping and give confidence to those who are interested.

L. Christian Schiller, CBE, MC, MA

8

Preface

This is not a book on Infant Method. There are many such books already and some are referred to or recommended in the text.

Our purpose has been to try to meet the demand for a 'book about Family Grouping', for which many people have asked. We have tried to examine not so much what *ought* to be done as what in fact is already being done, to present the reasons why those who teach in this way do so, what their aims and purposes are, and how they try to carry them out.

It may perhaps be useful to explain the terminology used in the title and in other places in the text.

'Family Grouping' is the familier name for Vertical All-Age grouping. The term 'Mixed-Age grouping' has been rejected as ambiguous. Many classes could be said to be composed of 'mixed' ages, particularly at the upper end of the Infants' school, where a form of streaming often prevails and young, intelligent children are promoted ahead of older, slower learners. Such classes are based on an absolute antithesis of Family Grouping principles—that is, they evaluate a child's progress in terms of intellectual attainment and move him about accordingly.

With deeper awareness of what true education involves, schools must try to look at a child not so much in terms of his intellectual performance as in terms of the person that he *is*. For this reason the chapters on children's development stand ordered as they do. The placing of chapters on emotional and social growth before that on the intellect is quite deliberate; emotional factors are of prime importance in the fulfilment and application of mental ability.

The repercussions of an individual's impact upon society, or that of society upon him, are of major significance in promoting mutual content and efficiency. For such reasons social development has been placed next.

This is not to belittle the importance of intellectual development, which, as it happens, has the longest chapter in the book.

Many readers will ask what it is that Family Grouping has to offer to children which more traditional systems cannot, or do not so easily, provide. The authors hope that the book will answer them. These following remarks on individual differences in children are pertinent:

"The importance of individual differences can scarcely be

over-estimated. Variations in innate mental ability account in part for some children being ready to learn reading, writing and arithmetic earlier than others. . . . Differences in home background and experience affect readiness for learning. . . . Some parents, happy and adjusted themselves, help their children to achieve emotional maturity; others, in bad relationships, produce a state of tension in the home which hampers the children's personal development."[1]

How is it possible for a teacher, knowing all this *in theory*, in practice to give the individual care which is needed by forty or so children whom she may know only for the space of a school year? It is not possible, and the attempt to do it imposes severe strain upon teachers—the more conscientious they are, the greater the strain. Some may ultimately respond by giving up the attempt, and may require children to conform to a standard pattern of behaviour and achievement, which is the negation of true education.

Teachers are important. They are a child's most valuable educational asset. Nothing can take their place—not splendid buildings, lavish equipment, television sets or teaching machines. And teachers, in the forseeable future, will still be in short supply. It is vital to use them in the best possible way.

To pass young children from teacher to teacher in their early years is surely not the best that can be done.

"The annual transfer of a group of children from class to class and from teacher to teacher is general in this country, but it appears to be based more on custom than on rational grounds."[2]

An ill-advised custom indeed: by this traditional transfer we squander the invaluable rapport which has built up between pupil and teacher, and which is highly prized from Nursery school to university. A child rarely undergoes fewer than two changes of teacher in his two or three years of Infants' school life, and it may well be more. We are imposing undesirable stresses on children *and* on their teachers, unnecessarily.

The authors have been struck by the atmosphere of happiness, confidence and serenity which characteristically pervades classroom after classroom of Family-grouped children. Such an atmosphere does not belong exclusively to Family-grouped classes, of course, but it is the regularity with which it occurs in them that makes it too marked to be coincidental.

"In a situation of personal security in relation to the adult, amongst companions with whom they may cooperate, offered experiences which stimulate thought and study, and with freedom to manipulate materials that are stimulating, manageable and satisfying, children learn to face, and progressively become able to solve, their problems.

---

[1] H. James and others: *Periods of Stress in the Primary School*.
[2] ibid.

Then, free from the internal stress which prevents development, they are able to use their energies to serve ends they desire and will; they are possessed of true and positive mental health."[1]

No one would suggest that such conditions do not prevail in some traditionally organized Infants' schools and classes, but it is the authors' view that they are more likely to be found in classrooms that are Family-grouped.

The authors gratefully acknowledge their indebtedness to the head-teachers and teachers of the schools listed below. Without visits to them, discussion with them, information and comment supplied by them, this book could not have been written.

Blaise C.P. Infants	Bristol
Bounds Green C.P. Infants	London Borough of Haringey
Broadhempston C.P. Junior Mixed and Infants	Devon
Dalmain C.P. Infants	ILEA
Downe C.P. Junior Mixed and Infants	Kent
Dusseldorf P. Infants	BFES
Eastbury Farm C.P. Junior Mixed and Infants	Hertfordshire
Elizabeth Lansbury Nursery School	ILEA
Erith C.P. Junior Mixed	Kent
Four Acres C.P. Infants	Bristol
Gordonbrock C.P. Infants	ILEA
Henbury Court C.P. Infants	Bristol
Herford P. Junior Mixed and Infants	BFES
Holbeton C.P. Junior Mixed and Infants	Devon
Laurence Weston C.P. Infants	Bristol
Loughborough C.P. Infants	ILEA
Meadow Vale C.P. Infants	Berkshire
Pakeman (formerly Shelbourne) C.P. Infants	ILEA
Plumberow C.P. Junior Mixed and Infants	Essex
Queen's Park C.P. Infants	ILEA
Royston C.P. Junior Mixed and Infants	London Borough of Bromley
St. Andrew's Infants	BAOR
St. John of Jerusalem C.P. Junior Mixed and Infants	ILEA
Sea Mills C.P. Infants	Bristol
Shipbourne C.P. Junior Mixed and Infants	Kent
Slapton C.P. Junior Mixed and Infants	Devon
Southcote C.P. Junior Mixed and Infants	Reading
Springfield C.P. Junior Mixed and Infants	ILEA
Stebon C.P. Infants	ILEA
Susan Lawrence C.P. Infants	ILEA
former William Forster C.P. Junior Mixed and Infants	London
Withywood C.P. Infants	Bristol

[1] W. Wall: *Education and Mental Health.*

Our special thanks are also due to Ludwick C.P. Infants' School, Herts, the first Family-grouped school we ever visited, and to Miss Parry, Inspector of Schools for Bristol.

As the authors are in the employ of the Borough of Bromley and the London Borough of Redbridge, it is necessary to state that the Councils of these Boroughs accept no responsibility for the opinions expressed in this book.

December 1964

Preface to the second edition

Since the first publication of this book the Department of Education and Science has issued a massive and inspiring report on the education of the primary school child – the Plowden Report.

There is in the Report little discussion of Family Grouping, referred to and indexed as 'Vertical Classification', although after four paragraphs (799 – 803), the report does state: "We have been impressed by the liveliness and good quality of the work in Infant Schools where classes extend over two or three age groups."

Neither is there reference to Vertical Classification at Junior level, but there is much discussion of allied aspects of modern thinking and practice, such as the emphasis on individual and group learning, incentives to learning, (it being noted of examinations that 'the children who most need the incentive of good marks are the ones least likely to gain them.'), and the fact that childrens' concept formation and clarification are facilitated by discussion with other children and with adults. Welcome is given to *un*streaming, and reference is made to a need for flexibility in organizing classes, with special discussion of the new trend towards team teaching. These are all matters relevant to Vertical Classification at Junior, or 'Middle' school level.

Since increasing experimentation with flexible age and ability groupings is in fact taking place and in response to many requests, we have added a chapter briefly describing the basis of this development, and the title of the book has been correspondingly modified.

The authors wish to pay tribute to, and to thank the teachers and headteachers of village and urban schools who have helped them to understand better the facts and philosophies associated with these trends.

April 1968

1

Family Grouping: What is it? Why do it?

The modern school is not an instrument simply for the training of the mind: it is not purely a machine of instruction: it is more and more consciously seen to be an institution which reflects and thus perpetuates and shapes the entire social group in which it exists.[1]

Traditional Age-grouping

On entering an Infants' school where Traditional class organization is used, a 5-year-old child is normally placed in the Reception class, which will probably contain from 35 to 40 other new entrants. Here he may spend from one to three terms. Transfer to the 'next class up' follows either at the age of 6 years, when a first full year has been completed, or earlier if a new intake of children at the following term or terms causes pressure.

Between the ages of 6 and 7 years a further transfer usually occurs to the 'top' or equivalent class where the Infant completes the first stage of his education before passing into the Junior school.

There are many variations of this basic pattern. Infants' schools seldom find that the new intake of 5-year-olds arrives in a neat bundle of 35 to 40. A few children sometimes go straight into the second class, and miss the Reception class altogether.

A re-shuffle often occurs at the beginning of each term, when a proportion of some or all classes moves up the school to make room for a few children from below.

Teachers dislike this system, since there is an inevitable trend towards losing their most mature and academically successful pupils before the conclusion of the academic year. In such circumstances a limited form of streaming is almost unavoidable, with young intelligent pupils passing ahead of older, duller ones. In some schools, this living moving staircase is so organized that many children keep the same teacher throughout their Infants' school career, and such planning gives a degree of stability to an otherwise disruptive procedure.

In yet other schools, teachers remain in set positions (often in the Reception or the 'top' class) and the children pass successively through their hands.

Should numbers require it, a new class of Reception or older children

---

[1] W. Wall: *Education and Mental Health.*

may be formed at the term beginning in January, or after Easter. A temporary teacher is usually in charge, who may or may not be familiar with the locality, or the teaching methods of the school.

Such are the basic patterns of the traditionally organized school.

Family Grouping

In a school where Family Grouping is used, a child remains in the same class, with the same teacher, for the whole period of his Infants' school life.

Entering with a few (perhaps 5 to 8 other newcomers), he joins a class which will already contain 10 to 12 children of rising 6-year-olds, and a further 10 to 12 rising 7-year-olds, all of whom have spent their Infants' school life up to that point in the same classroom taught by the same teacher (unless there have been staff changes).

Each 5-year-old is placed with a relative or friend. Often there is an older member of the family at school; there may be a cousin, or another child from the same street or block of flats whom he has met and played with outside school. Should he know no one at all in the Infant department (a fairly unusual circumstance) he is placed in the special care of an older, stable member of the class. There are likely to be several aspirants for this responsible task, which is always eagerly

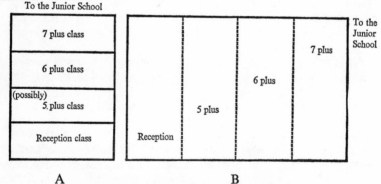

A TRADITIONAL AGE-GROUPING
  A child progresses through several classes according to his age (and possibly his ability)

B VERTICAL AGE-GROUPING
  A child remains in one class; his progress occurs within the framework of the class, and all classes are similarly formed

14

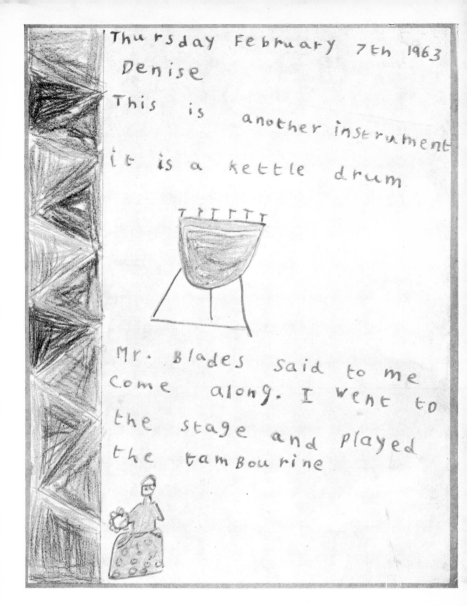

Thursday February 7th 1963
Denise

This is another instrument it is a kettle drum

Mr. Blades said to me come along. I went to the stage and played the tambourine

Page from a class "Book of Percussion Instruments"

Sound travels through wood

I konw Sound can travels through wood. because I have heared tryed it I heard a boy crayoning and I could not hear it very wdl So I Put my ear on the end of a wooden table. and I heard it better.

Page from one child's "Book of Sound"

sought and conscientiously discharged. All classes in the school are organized in this same way, and each is of equal 'status'.

At the end of each scholastic year, 7-year-olds, a dozen or so from every class, will transfer to the Junior school, leaving room for the new intake of 5-year-olds, who will filter in at the beginning of each term as they reach their appropriate entry age.[1]

The two methods can be represented as on previous page.

Why Do it?

At first sight Vertical Age-grouping may appear to add to the Infant teacher's already complex and exacting task a new dimension of difficulty—that of dealing in one class with three distinct age-levels, with all the variety of ability and stages of development in them, instead of with one age or ability level.

In practice teachers find that the system gives to the children a valuable sense of security and stability, and to their teacher a deeper quality of insight into their all-round development and character which springs from 2 to 3 years of close and intimate association.

A Child's Eye View

Let us return to a child entering for the first time the lively world of the Infants' school: consider through his eyes the unaccustomed size of its rooms, the lengths of corridors, the bewildering number of doors, windows, tables, chairs, coat pegs, lavatories, books and equipment, the gaunt playground bustling with vigorous life, and above all, the overwhelming number of other children, most of whom are bigger and familiar with their routine, rights, privileges and restrictions. The children like himself in the Reception class are all equally bewildered, immature and insecure, needing the reassurance of the one rather harassed teacher. In some instances the school may not be totally unfamiliar. Some Infants' schools arrange for preliminary visits before a child actually starts. But in any event, "the child's first experience of primary school" will be, in Dr. Wall's own word—"crucial".[2]

Children are resilient beings. Not all are anxious or apprehensive (though without doubt many are, as tears, thumb-sucking, reluctance to go to school, bed-wetting and other adjustment problems testify). Only a few cry on the first day and fewer still on subsequent days; most keep their anxieties to themselves, and appear to acquire quickly

---

[1] This varies according to the time of the year and the practice of the Local Education Authority. At the beginning of the first term of the year (Autumn) most L.E.A's allow 'rising 5's' to enter; i.e. those who will be 5 before Christmas. Some of these children will enter as young as 4 years 9 months. Thereafter many children have to wait until the beginning of the term after their fifth birthday. For those born in May or June, this may mean that they are 5 years and 3 or 4 months old before their schooling starts.

[2] W. Wall: *Education and Mental Health.*

a sense of confidence and of belonging, helped by the allocation of a special cloakroom peg, a certain place at a table, or a personal box of possessions kept in an individual place.

Within the space of one to three terms, a child in the traditionally organized school moves on to the next class, and begins all over again. He may or may not keep the same teacher: he is unlikely to stay in the same room. He knows the school now, but he faces new classroom conditions and a new daily régime.

It is worth noting that the length of time for which he has been 'settled' may vary from 60 to 200 days (School terms may be 12, 13 or 14 weeks of 5 days each, and the school year is 200 days only.) It should also be remembered that absences for minor or major illnesses, for holidays or other reasons, make periods of irregular attendance a normal part of Infants' school life and may cut the total drastically.

However, with rare exceptions, he must now move on.

Teachers vary in the extent to which they play upon the importance of 'going up'. Even though today there is increased awareness of the variability of natural maturation, and greater understanding of the extent to which anxieties and emotional stress influence intellectual performance, it is lamentably common for the encouragement of 'going up' or the implied stigma of 'staying down' to be used as a spur to intellectual effort or as an incentive to behavioural conformity.

Transfer time has been rightly referred to as the 'annual upheaval of moving up'; it imposes a physical and mental strain on teachers and children.

Bertrand Russell writes, "a life of uncertainty is nervously exhausting at all times, but especially in youth".[1] A school child's transfer from class to class is inevitably associated with a period of uncertainty: the unspoken unease ("Shall I be going up?"), the home pressure ("When are you going up?"), the reluctance, verbalized or suppressed ("I don't want to leave my teacher"), and the half-apprehensive curiosity about the new class teacher ("What's she like?") all build into the transfer situation a tension which can range from excited anticipation to regret or real fear.

It may be argued that children like to feel they are 'getting on', and that the pressure to do well in order to go up can be a useful stimulus. To which a pertinent reply might be "stimulus to what?" (see pages 61, 79).

Tensions and stress are an inevitable part of life. To what extent should they be minimized for young children? Do we, in minimizing them, help to achieve the objects of Infant's school education? These issues will be further discussed in Chapters 3, 4 and 5.

Traditional Age-grouping provides an Infants' school life of 2 to 3

---

[1] B. Russell: *Education and the Social Order*.

years in which there may be one, two or three transfers to new classes, with all the possible attendant emotional, social and intellectual disturbance. Coming to school is a tremendous event in itself, requiring a high degree of adjustment to new situations and people; perhaps the only comparable situation is that of starting in one's first job, and most adults will recollect only too vividly the feelings of apprehension and anxiety produced by this situation despite their greater maturity.

The transfer of a child from the class in which he is securely and happily settled without doubt acts as a break on his progress and emotional stability. Regression *always* occurs at change, as countless teachers have unwittingly testified in post-holiday comments. "They don't seem to remember a thing"; "I went over all that with them last term"; or, "Whatever has Miss Y been doing with them?" By contrast, the Family-grouped class has, from the first day, a most comforting degree of security to offer.

When the 5-year-old arrives, there is almost always another child known to him in the class, often an older brother or sister. He has heard at home about the teacher and about what happens in school; his mother knows her and he has probably been to the classroom door to collect the sibling; and he may have been welcomed inside. There is no traumatic situation, for much is familiar and the room contains a focal point of safety.

A young class teacher has said, "From the shelter of the more mature class-mate a new entrant can observe the teacher, sum up the new situations and become familiar with class and school routine; be helped to find his way to toilet, cloakroom, hall and playground; have personal attention *at the moment of need* to the comparative trivialities of shoelace-tying, buttoning and unbuttoning, milk-drinking and other little matters which, multiplied thirty to forty times, make such harassing demands upon the teacher, but which loom so large in importance to a young child fresh from the protection of home and the ready availability of his mother's help."

Tears are virtually unknown; adjustment is swift, for the 5-year-old enters a classroom atmosphere already ordered and stable, with two-thirds of the class fully established in the teacher's ways, and the teacher herself able to give time and attention to making, with a comparatively small number of newcomers, a relationship which she knows will have time to grow and mature over the next two to three years.

There are no more upheavals. With entry into school a period of social, emotional and intellectual development begins which, continuing unbroken through Infants' school life, builds into a child's personality a poise, enjoyment and confidence upon which his future Junior and Secondary schooling may depend.

To conclude this chapter which has briefly contrasted Traditional and Vertical Age-grouping, and at the same time to outline some of the purposes of the chapters which follow, the authors here suggest what appear to them to be the advantages of the Family Grouping system, and present some of the arguments for and against it.

Arguments For

1. Security and Progress

The first and most obvious benefit of Family Grouping is that a child who has once made the adjustment from home to school life can go steadily forward, growing in confidence, in physical and mental stature, without unnecessary checks, in an atmosphere which is more relaxed and serene for teacher and child because of the absence of pressures to prepare for the next 'move up'.

Some periods of regression inevitably occur in every child as a result of absence, illness, sibling jealousies, domestic instability, or inadequacies within the school itself. They are minimized, because the teacher has a prolonged acquaintance with each one of her pupils. Knowing a pupil better, and therefore appreciating his difficulties more thoroughly, she can help him through unstable periods, and tolerate without undue anxiety his fluctuations of attainment or behaviour (see Chapter 3).

2. Mutual Aid

The effect of the help which children consciously and unconsciously give to each other is immeasurable.

It has far-reaching repercussions on social and intellectual development (see Chapters 4 and 5); it stimulates the development of spoken language; it ranges from the half-conscious absorption of knowledge through incidental overhearing to the deliberate teaching of younger by older children of skills such as reading, or of training in putting out and clearing away equipment. It may take the form of imitation of the more mature behaviour of an older member of the class, or it may provide opportunity for an older child to show thoughtfulness to a younger one or to reinforce his own grasp of a skill by teaching it.

Responsibility and independence developed in the older children are transmitted to younger ones, who in their turn pass the benefits they have received to newer arrivals.

It is no exaggeration to say that, in the Family-grouped classroom, already stable and content, the older children really look forward to the coming of new 5-year-olds and treat them with great kindness and consideration.

Referring to the maturation of intelligence with increasing age, Wheeler comments that, "the main influence is the child's free intercourse with other children, particularly when the latter vary in age and understanding",[1] and this is borne out by the evidence of teachers working in Family-grouped classrooms.

3. *Lightening the Teacher's Load*

Because of the help which the children give to each other, and because the groups of varying ages are not too large, pressure on the class teacher is proportionately eased.

The 5-year-olds, relaxed and confident, can play together, and are not too numerous to receive their due amount of individual attention, which is almost impossible when the Reception class numbers 40 or more. Every Infants' teacher knows the urgency in the voice of the 6-year-old who has just found the pleasures of reading, and who persistently asks, "Can you hear me now?" She reluctantly says, "I will— but later on", as she faces the impossible task of hearing the whole class, all at approximately the same critical and dependent stage together. The strain is eased when only one third of the class needs that particular kind of individual help. Learning is correspondingly faster. The purposeful learning of the more mature 7-year-olds can be harnessed for longer and more profitable periods of time (see Chapter 2).

The pace of the day is altogether more leisurely, particularly where active and self-directed methods of learning are used; such methods lend themselves naturally to individual growth, to initiative and cooperation, and the undesirable element of competition for the teacher's attention and for her approval is at a minimum (see Chapter 4). The personal methods which every teacher develops are given their fullest value, as their continuity is assured over the whole of the infant's school life. As she gets to know the children better, the teacher gains insight into their individual development and can foster the all-round progress of each.

Says Nathan Isaacs, "All the work done by Piaget . . . has only served to increase the force and weight of his picture of slow, inward, evolutionary growth," and further, "What is involved is the degree of contrast there can be between the cumulative action of consistently unfavourable circumstances, or averagely mixed ones, and conditions that are expressly planned, with full understanding and insight, to be the most favourable ones possible."[2]

We strongly suggest that a stable relationship with his teacher, built up over a long period, is one of the favourable circumstances most urgently needed by a young child; at the same time, the teacher is herself not called upon to get to know, or to consider the needs of, 30 to 40 new children all at once, or to build up her classroom atmosphere from scratch each year.

---

[1] D. Wheeler: *Studies in the Development of Reasoning in School Children.*
[2] N. Isaacs: *Some Aspects of Piaget's Work.*

Teachers speak of the gain in community spirit amongst themselves. Each deals with the full range of Infants' school ages, and profitable discussion of problems common to all is stimulated. No one feels, "Here is a difficulty for the Reception class teacher to solve," or "This only applies to the top class." All have the satisfaction of witnessing the blossoming of intellectual capacities most clearly seen at the upper end of the school.

4. *Variations in Personal Growth*

Allowance can be made for individual differences and fluctuations in every aspect of children's personality.

Teachers are well aware that chronological and mental ages do not necessarily correspond; it is not so well recognized that there are other variations of equal importance to consider.

The young, intellectually able child may be quite immature emotionally; the slow learner who is well behind in intellectual attainment may be very stable and well adjusted socially. Such children have much to offer one another. With others of similar uneven development they can merge inconspicuously into the work and play groups which best suit their level of development.

The same child, at different times subjected to different stresses, such as a period of ill-health or the arrival of the new baby, makes use of the wide range of work and play situations available to work through his temporary regressions or fluctuating interests. It is easy to recapture a forgotten stage of learning, to use toys or equipment normally provided for younger children, and try out mental skills of the stage beyond and not be dismayed by failure, because all these situations exist in one and the same classroom; work and play groups form naturally, crystallize and disintegrate; each member contributes what he can and takes what he needs from the interaction of personality, judgment and intellect in the wide spectrum of capacities present in the same class.

What Susan Isaacs called the "basic spontaneous interests of children" (page 27) can all be catered for: children are free to find their own level without restraint, and to fluctuate upwards or downwards according to their own need.

5. *School-Home Cooperation*

With long-term development in mind, and the grouping of members of the same family within the same class, the opportunity for cooperation between parent and teacher is very marked.

The majority of parents like the system once they understand it (see Chapter 9). Mothers feel at home with a teacher they get to know well, and regard her as a friend who has the interests of each child at heart. They are pleased for their children to be together once they know that each member of the class goes on learning at his own pace.

Teachers get to know and understand a mother's problems and difficulties and can often offer advice on matters relating to children's growth and behaviour. Children are particularly vulnerable to differences of opinion between home and school, and they feel an increased confidence in the knowledge that there is cooperation between them.

Some Arguments Against

1. *Strain on the Teacher*

It has been suggested that the strain on the teacher will be impossibly severe in keeping groups of children purposefully occupied at such widely divergent stages of learning. Opinions have been voiced that "the 5-year-olds will be neglected" or "the 7-year-olds will not be stretched". In practice it is found that such fears are not justified.

Since within the class of 40 children of a single age-group there will in any case be a wide range of intellectual ability (and emotional and social development too), the work in the Infants' school must always be graded to suit individual and group needs. It is no more difficult to do this for a Vertically-grouped than for a Traditionally-grouped class.

The teacher is relieved of much of the tedious but essential training associated with the care of equipment and materials, since newcomers learn by imitation. There is always a group of experienced children to guide the others; routine tasks are performed more quickly and easily, and time is saved.

Discussion or group teaching can take place with 12 to 14 children at a time (the largest number in any case with whom children normally make social contact), and if such occasions are fewer than with a whole class of one age, they will certainly, because of the smaller size of the group, be more effective.

A teacher undergoing personal stress of any kind can be helped by the reduction of the intake of entrants in any term; they may be distributed amongst the other classes—a simple way of keeping classes smaller. This is not always possible in a Traditionally-grouped school. Similar modifications can be made for particularly small classrooms or for the inexperienced or elderly teacher.

2. *Personality Clashes*

It has been suggested that personality clashes between teacher and child, or between siblings, may make it undesirable for children to spend 2 to 3 years in the same class.

Discord between teacher and child which cannot be resolved is rare indeed, but if it should occur it can be overcome by putting the child in another class. As all classes are structurally alike this is the simplest matter possible. So far from sibling rivalries being intensified, in almost all cases the opposite occurs. Where harm might be done to any child, or where parents particularly wish it (as in cases of identical twins), a suitable place in another class can always be found.

3. *Noise*

The problem of noise, in particular of disturbance of older children at work by the play of the younger ones, has been postulated, but here again it turns out in practice that with proper forethought these fears prove groundless. The 5-year-olds are frequently the least noisy group; older children are easier to control because they are fewer in number than in a class all of one age, and they are aware of the special position of responsibility they hold.

As one teacher light-heartedly observed, "There's never any problem with discipline," and this partly arises from the fact that each child is developing naturally at his own pace.

Periods of tranquillity and quiet occupation are essential for educational purposes at all levels; the purposeful work of the Family-grouped class goes on in an atmosphere of serenity and composure in which all children can pursue their personal tasks with undisturbed concentration.

4. *Expense*

The expense of equipping a whole school along Family-grouped lines has often been queried. In fact, initially the cost is probably greater than that of equipping a more traditional school. Each class-room needs the equipment usually found in the Reception class—sand tray, water tray, domestic play corner, large building bricks, and so on. General equipment must be available for all levels: there must for instance be jigsaw puzzles suitable for the youngest and oldest child in each class; books and number equipment will be needed for every attainment level in every class. The quantities required, however, will be proportionately smaller, and the overall cost little greater.

There is no difference whatever in maintenance costs, and there is the inestimable advantage that suitable toys, books, equipment and apparatus are at hand whenever each child needs them.

5. *Class Teaching*

How can you give a lesson in Music, Physical Education, or Religious Education to the whole class when the ages of the children vary so widely? What about choosing stories or poems that are suitable for children of 5 and 7 years?

The difficulties posed by such questions are not as insurmountable as might at first appear. Indeed, there are at times positive advantages for the children in taking part in such class lessons with a mixed age-group.

Both advantages and disadvantages are dealt with subject by subject in Chapter 6.

2

Aims and Purposes: Ways and Means

A scheme of education is ultimately to be valued by its success in fostering the highest degrees of individual excellence of which those submitted to it are capable.[1]

Aims and Purposes

Schools are kaleidoscopic: no two are alike, and very few schools remain the same for long at a time. The children, the adults, the equipment, the teaching techniques undergo a constant shift; patterns of acceptable behaviour are drawn and redrawn; modes of thinking and ways of learning suffer continual modification as schools reflect the changing demands of society, the increased understanding of children's needs and their mental functioning.

The teacher is part of this change, yet she must also be able to look at it objectively. Allied to flexibility of mind, she needs a sense of ultimate purpose as the virtues of one method are debated and weighed against those of another.

Is there a target for her—an 'end product' at which to aim? Does it really make all that difference how classes are arranged, or skills taught?

Books on education proliferate, training becomes longer, and opportunities for in-service study and discussion increase. Teachers begin to feel that they have a pretty good idea what *should* be done. Here is a splendid summary by Edna Mellor: "My philosophy of education is concerned with the whole child—his physical, mental and spiritual growth; his feelings, attitudes and relationships; his character and personality. It is concerned with him as an individual having certain innate tendencies, potentialities and traits, and also with him as a member of society having certain rights and privileges, duties and responsibilities."[2] This springs from a noble educational ancestry from Plato, through Rousseau, Pestalozzi, Froebel, Dewey, Montessori and others whose views have intermarried with those of other philosophers and educationalists of insight and experience: it reflects the high aspiration of most Infants' teachers—to give opportunity for the best possible growth to every child.

---

[1] P. Nunn: *Education: Its Data and First Principles.*
[2] E. Mellor: *Education through Experience in the Infants' School Years.*

But the means to this end may not be unanimously agreed. Whatever may be their views about ultimate aims, or the means of arriving at them, Infants' schools share a common starting-point—a child as he *is*, in all his variability, curious and eager to explore the world, timid or aggressive, uninhibited or limited in self-expression, not docile perhaps, but powerfully activated to investigate and to find out for himself. For this last quality schools should rejoice, though they may find it a little difficult to encourage this attribute when there are 40 or more zealous investigators around one teacher.

Methods and Motivation for Learning

With the optimum growth of each child as the teacher's aim, how can she best achieve such a purpose with the varied human material before her?

There is probably no one answer, and certainly no one panacea or teaching technique that will eliminate all problems. Vertical Age-grouping lays no claim to this. But there are three priorities which would seem to emerge, and which Family Grouping does help to promote.

Firstly, recognizing that investigating and learning are inherent and basically satisfying to *all* children, our purpose in school must be to see that learning keeps this inherent attraction, not only for the most able but for all children.

Secondly, we must help the young learner from his earliest years to help himself so that he does not wait passively for instruction but actively pursues the matters which interest him: we must instruct where need be but make the pursuit of further learning partly his own responsibility. We can never teach all there is to know: the horizon always recedes. We cannot envisage all that the children we are teaching may need to know. "These children look forward into a future that we shall not share."[1] An attitude of self-help in the Infant will stand him in good stead all his life; but he is more likely to think learning worth while if it furthers an interest spontaneously born within him.

We must regard a child, even an Infants' school child, as a student and investigator at all levels, place him in situations which interest him—even excite him—equip him as he needs them with the tools for advancing his knowledge, and never, never blur his vision of learning as being something both desirable and enjoyable.

Thirdly, we must be continually alive to the possibility that our teaching methods may not be developing a child's full potential: we must constantly assess and reassess children's successes and failures in terms of the competence of the teaching or of the school environment.

---

[1] R. Griffiths: *A Study of Imagination in Early Childhood.*

"Many a failure attributed to the pupil is in fact a failure in the curriculum, the method or the teacher."[1]

We must remember to accept the child always as he is, not as we think he ought to be, develop his full potential at each appropriate level, and retain in him the zest for learning natural to the young of all species. These maxims seem simple enough, yet they present an awesome challenge.

How many adults can say that they have developed, or even hope to develop, their full potential abilities, especially bearing in mind that development of personality embraces far more than the cultivation of intellectual capacity?

What goes to the making of the happy and efficient human being? A list of attributes would certainly include poise, humour, tolerance, sensitivity and creativity—which can all begin their effective growth in the Infants' school child.

What is implied in the expression 'full potential abilities'? We do not know. Although teachers now do know with greater certainty than they ever did (thanks to the intensive and scientific child study of Gesell, Piaget, Susan and Nathan Isaacs, Valentine, Schonell, Vernon, Stern, Burt and many others) how to arrange appropriate conditions for children's development, and have greater insight into the stages of mental and physical maturation[2] upon which such development depends, there are few teachers bold enough to predict for any child what might be his final ceiling of attainment, or at what age he may attain it.

Experience suggests that we stand only on the threshold of awareness of the conditions which need to be fulfilled before every child is functioning at his maximum potential. There are schools imaginatively and purposefully planned, wisely equipped and staffed by teachers confident enough to free their pupils from unnecessary restrictions, and sensitive enough, whilst placing children in stimulating situations, to leave them alone until a moment of need arises, when they come forward with the teaching of some further skill, or place at the child's disposal their own wider knowledge and broader vision, indicating where further investigation may lead, or where more information may be obtained.

Such schools and teachers have been astonished and delighted at the width of interests shown by little children, at the persistence and industry with which they pursue them, and the heights to which, in language, artistic, musical and other spheres, young children's creativity will rise. Such successes make such methods self-perpetuating. No teacher having experienced these rewards will lightly discard the means by which they have been obtained.

---

[1] W. Wall, F. Schonell, W. Olson: *Failure in School.*
[2] "Slow inward evolutionary growth." (Nathan Isaacs).

25

On the other hand, there are teachers who look dubiously at the dull pupil, perhaps conscientiously prodding him into some routine learning task, and wonder where evidence is to be found of the built-in curiosity, the desire and capacity for self-education, the inquiring spirit which is said to be concealed underneath that stolid exterior; perhaps a little of it might be glimpsed as the child comes to life in the crowded city street, investigating the possibilities for play in a scrap heap at the corner, or leading small friends in imaginative games of battle in forbidden places.

How can schools best harness this inborn initiative, curiosity and drive for learning? In the words of L. A. Reid, "The child possesses the 'potency'; the teacher is *one factor* in the change from 'potency' to 'fulfilment'."[1]

The task of the schools is to release this 'potency' and encourage it to operate to the full. It exists in every child, from the dullest to the most able: its manifestation will vary according to personality and *opportunity*.

Susan Isaacs summarizes the schools' task as follows: "For me, the school has two functions: (a) to provide for the child's own bodily and social skills and means of expression, and (b) to open the facts of the external world (the real external world that is, not the school 'subjects') to him in such a way that he can seize them and understand them."[2]

Her valuable book demonstrates clearly that, so far from there being any incompatibility between children following their own impulses and interests and the mastery of the tool subjects which have constituted the traditional curriculum of Infants' Schools (and concerning which there is evidence of anxiety in public places today[3]), the two will blend and intermingle in the hands of the alert and skilful teacher, each reinforcing and enlivening the other. Educational journals, books and reports abound with the evidence of such lively and skilful teaching.

Play and 'Activity' Methods

When a young child pursues his own pleasures and interests, such activity is commonly called 'play', and the importance of play for physical and mental health is now so positively established as to be beyond refuting. It has long been agreed that children work better if they have periods of play and relaxation. But many teachers now realize that 'work' and play can be so intertwined as to become one.

The 'play way' and 'activity' methods have in some quarters fallen

---

[1] L. Reid: *Philosophy and Education.*

[2] S. Isaacs: *Intellectual Growth in Young Children.*

[3] A typical example is that of newspaper reports (August 1964) of complaints by the British Employers Confederation that young employees lack 'a good grasp of the 3 Rs'.

into disrepute because, misunderstood, they have led to wasted time and opportunity, to frustration in children and exhaustion in teachers.

Yet play, freely used, discloses starting-points of interest, and unfolds possibilities for extension through which children, aided at the right moment by their teacher, can experience their growing ability to find out more, the satisfaction of learning more and the excitement of seeing how much more there always is to know.

The National Union of Teachers has this to say of the skilled use of children's freely chosen pursuits: "It is interesting to note how inevitably children find their need of the 3 Rs. There is no antipathy towards the skills when they have meaning and purpose. If the need for them arises in their play, children apply themselves to learning with a keenness and determination that helps them overcome difficulties and makes for speedy and joyful learning. There is then more progress made in a few months than is usual in years by traditional methods, when teaching is so often given before interest arises."[1]

Gertrude Cooper, writing of the nature and value of children's play, says: "What transpires is a revelation to us of the way children's imaginations work, and of the ingenuity and resourcefulness shown in their wide range of play interests."[2]

In one Infants' class, at the end of the term, a little group of 6 and 7-year-old girls had turned out the dolls' drawers and washed and hung up several lines of dolls' clothes (a chore usually performed by teachers). The teacher stood watching a competent little 7-year-old who was seated safely in a barricaded corner ironing the dolls' bedding on a strong board. She said, "I was a bit dubious at first, but I'm glad I let them do it. They've proved they can. I think there are a lot of things children can do, if only we give them the opportunity. These children have washed and ironed a whole drawer full of clothes today."

In another school, a similar activity had led to the writing of laundry lists, the counting and sorting of garments, and dolls' boxes and drawers were being efficiently labelled.

The characteristic spontaneous activities of children of all ages are described by Susan Isaacs[3] as:

1. The perfecting of bodily skills, the joy in movement and control of movement for its own sake.

2. Make-believe play.

3. Investigation into physical things; into animals and plants; the satisfaction of intellectual curiosity.

A school treasuring, cultivating and using such interests may well be

---

[1] N.U.T. Report on Nursery-Infant Education.
[2] G. Cooper: *The Place of Play in an Infants' and Junior School.*
[3] S. Isaacs: *Intellectual Growth in Young Children.*

described as allowing children plenty of opportunity to 'play': it would be providing wide scope and strong motivation to learn.

Play is the instrument for intellectual growth, and one which lies ready-made for us to use. It is further discussed in Chapters 3, 4 and 5.

Activity Methods and Family Grouping

Assuming that in this way, when they do learn, children learn faster and take greater pleasure in their learning, that they retain their enthusiasm (that they are in fact ego-involved[1]) and that they also develop qualities of initiative and responsibility, in what way can it be said that Vertical Age grouping helps the organization of this way of learning?

The answer is simple: it reduces the demands made upon a teacher, and offers greater scope for a child to function at the level most needed by him at any particular moment.

With an age-range of 5 to 7 plus, stages of 'play' vary widely. Mature children enjoy organizing play situations; less mature ones need accept no more responsibility than they are ready to take. Dependent children look to more robust ones for support and help. This presents a natural outlet for the leader, the motherly and the socially well-developed child. Pressures on the teacher are lessened.

With an age-range of 5 to 7 plus, stages of 'work' vary widely too. Approximately one third of the class may enjoy play occupations for a large part of the day without the teacher having a nagging feeling that they "ought to be getting on". Another third (those whose interest in the intellectual skills of reading, writing or number has just been sparked off and who are at the most dependent stage of their learning life) has proportionately easier access to the teacher, and so makes more rapid progress. The most advanced children, now better able to help themselves, can work at tasks provided and planned to sustain their interest over longer periods, and yet still have access to equipment traditionally related to earlier levels if they should need it.

It may be that we underestimate the importance of the last point. In a school with one 'cell' class of Family-grouped children (see Chapter 8), a teacher relates that, owing to pressure on school places, all the other classes, even though not normally Vertically Age-grouped, took in the last term of the year a few new 5-year-old entrants. The 7-year-olds in these classes commented that they "liked playing with the little children's toys", and made special mention of the sand and water provision to which they no longer had access.

In the same school, two backward 6½ to 7-year-old boys were transferred from a Horizontally-grouped to the Family-grouped class,

---

[1] "The difference between real education and mere training may ultimately depend on the extent to which the individual is ego-involved." K. Lovell: *Educational Psychology and Children.*

their teacher commenting, "they'd play in the Home Corner all day if I let them". They would—and in the new class did, until they had exhausted this need.

Since it is well known that children discard without regret a plaything which has no further value for them, it is clear that the materials in the examples above filled some deep-seated need for these particular children.

Teachers with confidence in the ability of children to satisfy their own needs, given full opportunity, and with conviction that this is necessary in that it leads in the end to poise of personality and interest in more mature and abstract ways of learning, wholeheartedly refute the idea that children will "go on playing as long as you let them" (in the sense of 'wasting time'). Time is only wasted if the provision for play is inadequate. Emotional and social satisfaction pave the way to intellectual growth, provided the opportunities for progress are there.

As with adults, there is an ebb and flow in children's intellectual performance. Several teachers have mentioned the way in which an individual or a group, having worked with sustained effort over days or even weeks (as in the centre of interest on prehistoric animals described in Chapter 5), will show a need for relaxation and refreshment. The children mentioned here fell back on a self-initiated enthusiasm for plasticine modelling, and a fresh wave of interest in 'reading for pleasure'.

A Family-grouped classroom, with its wide range of materials and equipment, gives ample scope for individual choice, and opportunity to regress or pause when necessary.

The Daily Programme

If children are to work, even for part of the day, at self-selected pursuits, the highly organized class time-table must disappear. There can be few Infants' schools where the days are still disrupted into 20-minute or half hour spells of teaching activity. Most schools recognize that small children need large blocks of time which allow for careful preparation for a task, undisturbed pursuit of it, and unhurried clearing away. Their days are organized accordingly.

What is the *right* length of time for a child to work at his self-appointed, or his teacher-directed task? (Teacher-directed tasks are not incompatible with a general principle of learning based on children's play interests.)

The ideal length of time must surely be *as long as is needed until the interest is exhausted*. This may be half an hour, a morning, a day, a week, or longer. Many mothers are well aware that when young children want to do anything they want to do it *now*; and although it is undoubtedly part of the task of the adult to help a child to tolerate frustration and part of the maturation process of that child to learn to do so, the cultivation of the ability to concentrate for long spans of time is so valuable a quality for future learning that teachers should go to great lengths to avoid disrupting a naturally absorbing task.

Teachers who watch their pupils attentively soon become sensitive to their needs. A teacher said of a group of children who were involved in acting the same story day after day, "I thought I ought to stop the drama, but they seemed as though they needed it."

Gutteridge places first in her educational recommendations: "A child needs ample time and opportunity for completing his natural attention period."[1] But even a 'free' day must have a rhythm or pattern to it, and there are necessary class routines involving the use of the hall, or meal times, or other time-table requirements for which allowance must be made.

Children who know as a matter of regular consistent experience that they can return to work or play out a particular interest will put it aside quite happily for meals or other breaks. Teachers and head-teachers in their turn have devised simple yet flexible time-tables in order to give the maximum scope for child-involved activities to be pursued.

A very great deal of careful thinking has gone into the question of organizing Infants' schools programmes and environment. The authors recommend the books mentioned below for those interested in informed and imaginative discussion of varieties of daily programme.[2]

Such works as these, which are only a sample of the literature available on the subject, are full of practical help and deep understanding of children's and teachers' problems. They all agree that children's spontaneous activities provide the key to their mental and emotional health and growth. The methods described need skill, patience, love and faith on the part of teachers. The authors suggest that teachers actually find it easier, and not more difficult, as might be expected, to carry them out in Family-grouped classes.

The basis of time-tables described in such works is the allotment of large units of time for the following activities:

(a) playing and talking
(b) making and creating
(c) exploring and enlarging interests (some of which will first have shown themselves to the discerning teacher in (a) and (b))
(d) group discussion

---

[1] M. Gutteridge: *The Duration of Attention in Young Children.*
[2] D. Simpson and D. Alderson: *Creative Play in the Infants' School.*
  E. Mellor: *Education Through Experience in the Infants' School Years.*
  L. Sealey and V. Gibbon: *Communication and Learning in the Infants' School.*
  E. Boyce: *The First Year in School.*
  L. Hollamby: *Young Children Living and Learning.*

(e) teaching and practising the skills

(f) experience in the areas of culture—literature, music, religious education

(g) physical education

Descriptions of such Daily Programmes follow, taken from actual school situations. The first might be described as 'Partially Free', and is explained by the teacher who planned it for a fully Family-grouped class.

9.15–10.30 a.m.   Child-selected activity

drama, painting, creating, modelling, brick-building, sewing, clay, woodwork, water and sand play, domestic play (including cooking), creative music, classroom tasks such as seeing to fish, hamster, nature charts and discovery table, follow-through of interest work, self-chosen skills practice, picture books, number games, jigsaws.

Teacher's comments: "The children get out what they need, paint, clay and paste having already been prepared by me or some of the older children. Sometimes I get out things I think they have forgotten, or introduce a new idea—perhaps a fresh way to make puppets or people; but this is usually in response to a request for help. I am at the disposal of the children: I work around with them all the time. The children have limited access to a cloakroom or the outside where they can overflow to work or play. The reading corner is always extremely popular. The children come to school knowing what they want to do; it is very seldom a child does nothing unless he has just come to school and is looking round taking it all in."

10.30 a.m.   School prayers, followed by a staggered playtime (owing to lack of space in the playground)

11.0 a.m.   'Together' time—may be 5 or 30 minutes.

Teacher's comments: "This is the children's 'telling time'. We don't have any 'news' time as such. I think it's a bit artificial, and we never all write the same piece of news, but any special point of interest may be brought up for all to hear. It's my 'telling time' too, and I tell any school news or show a new book or piece of apparatus: there may be some special school function to talk about, or a reminder about behaviour. The children may talk about or show some piece of work they have done earlier in the morning. The children come together straight away and sit down. They seem to like this time. If the discussion is prolonged, the youngest children (and any others who are not really interested) may go off and play quietly."

11.20 a.m.   Skills—practise time

(a) for the youngest group, self-chosen activities as earlier

(b) for the middle group, free choice of skills work through the reading, writing and number corners

(c) for the most able, self-chosen or teacher-directed work in the tool subjects.

Teacher's comments: "Although there is self-chosen activity still going on, especially for the youngest, the children know that consideration must be shown to those who are 'working' and noise is kept to a minimum. As much as possible of the 3 Rs work stems from centres of interest or discovery based on the early morning choices. The skills work of each child is based on his choice, ability and progress and may not reflect his chronological age: i.e. younger able children can work with the oldest group, and slow older children may choose simple tasks or play activities. Pressure is avoided, but the children seem to want to get on; they ask for help. No one seems to want to be 'lazy'. Group work may occur if it happens that several children need special instruction at the same time, e.g. phonics for the older ones, flash cards or oral number. I help all groups but the children know that this is a time when I give special individual help in reading and so on. There might occasionally be class work, e.g. each child making a picture or other contribution for a class magazine, or all working for some special function such as Christmas. Any child very much absorbed in an early morning task knows he can carry it through till it is complete."

12.0 noon.	'Together' time for Religious Education
12.15 p.m.	Dinner-time
1.45–2.45 p.m.	As for period 11.20–12.0 noon, interspersed through the week with class periods for Physical Education or Music
2.45–3.0 p.m.	Afternoon break
3.0–3.45 p.m.	'Together' time for story and poetry.

Many teachers arrange their programme like this. Others prefer the following 'Free (or Integrated) Day'.

The Free (or Integrated) Day

This programme again arranges broad units of time, but there is no differentiation between children's self-chosen activities, play, projects, centres of interest, creative work, and practice in the tool subjects.

The teachers who work in this way feel, in the words of one, that, "these aspects of experience all impinge upon one another," and that "children recognize little difference between congenial work and play". They know that children will cheerfully practice reading, writing or number if there is strong enough motivation.

Here is an account, written by an outside observer, of a Transitionally-grouped (see Chapter 8) class in London working a Free Day:

"The teacher provided every type of activity imaginable—clay,

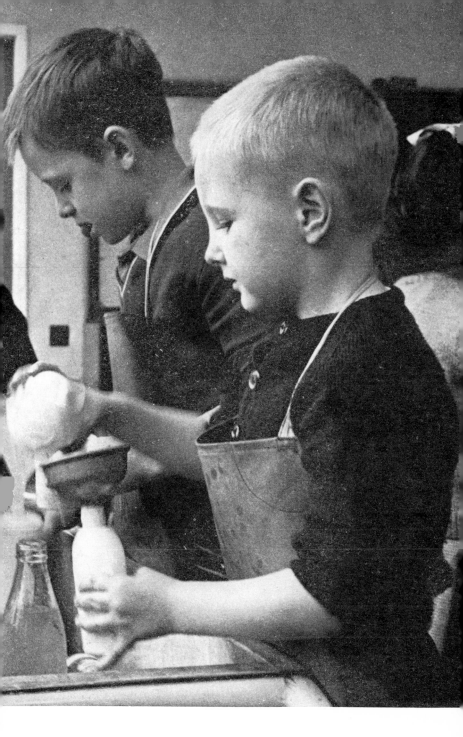

Children of 5 and 7 years at water-play

Two children of 6 and 7 years at number work together

paint, sand, water, papier mâché, sewing, woodwork and so on. All materials were available for the children's use throughout the whole day. There was no artificial splitting up of the day for different types of activity. Not knowing the children it was impossible for me to sort out the youngest from the oldest. They all seemed to be mixing freely and happily together. A few of the children were busy writing their own news.

"The class teacher said that she encouraged them to do some reading, writing and number work each day, but she was not insistent on this if she felt that they had been working hard on some other interest. She felt that over a period, the time spent on the basic skills evened itself out and that on the whole the children's natural enthusiasm was sufficient to ensure that the amount of time spent on the basic skills was adequate.

"All teaching was done on an individual basis, apart from the teaching of phonics to a small group of the older children towards the end of the academic year. In this school no critic of modern methods could say that freedom for the children had resulted in poor standards of work."

Due time must be allocated to Music, Religious Education, Physical Education and Story-time (see Chapter 6). But in some schools where the Free Day is practised, no special time is set aside for milk drinking. The milk is placed upon an attractively prepared 'milk-table', with cover and flowers, and the children help themselves when they wish. In some areas again the artificial 'playtime' break for children has been abandoned. The children have free access to the open air, and not having been penned up at classroom tables, have no need of 'liberating' exercise. A coffee break is made possible for teachers by cooperation with colleagues or by using school helpers for temporary supervision.

It is interesting to note, in connection with the Free Day, that Susan Isaacs states of the Maltinghouse school:

"The general method of the school aimed at cultivating the children's own active efforts in as many directions as possible." But, "this free activity had its necessary practical limits, and was set in a general framework of relatively fixed events."[1]

Unsuitable classrooms, large classes and changing staff sometimes discourage teachers and headteachers from attempting freer régimes, especially the full Free Day which some might like to try.

Family Grouping is helpful here because:
1. Every class is small at the beginning of the year; this makes it a good time for experimenting.
2. As all classes are alike, the activities of one class do not disturb another's.

---

[1] S. Isaacs: *Intellectual Growth in Young Children.*

3. After the first reorganization has been made there is always a proportion of the class familiar with the storage system of apparatus
   and equipment, experienced in its care and with the routine of the
   teacher. Since the essence of the free classroom and self-directed
   work is that children shall undertake responsibility for much of
   their own work and play, it is imperative that they be well trained
   in the techniques of caring for books and materials. The task of
   training the class afresh each year takes heavy toll of a teacher's
   time and patience (and sometimes of the materials in question!)
   With Family Grouping it only has to be done once. Each year the
   older children take over much of the responsibility and with reinforcing help from the teacher teach the younger ones in their
   turn.

An experienced headteacher has this to say on how to begin the
Free Day: "Divide your room into four corners—reading, writing,
creative and number. Make your class into four groups. Each day
move them round, so that they begin each day in a different corner.
Groups will soon break up. Children can soon begin to take responsibility for each day doing a daily assignment of work. Prepare well
in advance. Have plenty for the children to do, and a wide range of
assignment cards or books in Discovery work and the 3 Rs. You'll
never look back."

Classroom and School Buildings
   Only those who are subjected to them can know how profoundly the
conditions in which children and teachers have to work will influence
the quality of their performance.

The National Union of Teachers has evidence of unsuitable and
insanitary school conditions which should shame this affluent society
and give it cause to consider how much potential talent in teachers and
children goes to waste for lack of better working conditions.

E. R. Boyce[1] paints an unhappy picture of the dirty, depressing,
discouraging and restricting conditions in which small children still
work, play, or eat their meals. Yet with almost disconcerting initiative,
courage and gaiety teachers and taught contrive to rise above the sor-
didness of some of their working conditions and reach inspiring levels
of excellence and originality in creative work and the tool subjects.

Basic requirements are well understood by architects (who are
developing the most enlightened attitudes about the functional suita-
bility of school buildings), by Local Education Authorities who plan
and direct, and even by the general public.

Examples can be seen in Bristol, Oxfordshire, Leicestershire, Hert-
fordshire and many other areas of 'workshop' classrooms, of interest-

---

[1] E. Boyce: *The First Year in School.*

34

ing and useful shapes with adjacent toilet and cloakroom facilities, quiet bays or corners, and access to a terrace or garden work/play area. They are splendid and inspiring places for those who work in them, but there are not enough of them. Most children and teachers have to make do with something older and of less appropriate design.

We suggest the following ways in which the ordinary run-of-the-mill classroom could be transformed into the modern 'workshop' appropriate for all-round child development:

1. Creation of means of access to the outside. Comparatively cheap and easy to do for many classrooms; it may mean only knocking a hole in a wall and putting in a door, or dropping a window to floor level. This would be a comparatively cheap way of adding to classroom space and making sun and air available, and of helping the teacher to adopt a permissive attitude to woodwork noise, creative music-making or dramatic play, as sounds disperse so much more easily in the open air.[1]

2. Provision of running water and a sink in every classroom. This may be fairly expensive, but pays splendid dividends in enlarging the possibilities and convenience for painting and handwork, for understanding some aspects of number and science; for nature work and pet care—not to speak of everyday hygiene.

3. Placing of corridor/cloakroom/cubby-hole space at the children's disposal for big brick or other play. Expense—nil. Many schools have circulation space which is not yet fully utilized.

4. Fixing of long chalking board to corridor walls at children's level. Expense—minimal.

5. Provision of large flat storage space at children's level for their possessions. Most of the drawers, tidy boxes and pigeon-hole cupboards provided for Infants are too narrow for proper storage of their larger books. Tray-type individual drawers need only be shallow; deeper group-storage boxes could contain larger equipment. The ingenuity which teachers display in making or providing boxes, cartons, cardboard or wooden containers, is most admirable —but appallingly wasteful in time and effort. A muddled, confused classroom is a bad example daily before the children's eyes; as a work-place it should not be expected to be meticulously neat, but many are unnecessarily untidy for lack of suitable storage space.

---

[1] There are other advantages. "Children who are free to move about in a classroom, and to undertake play activities and occupations . . . are very different in the way they conduct themselves upon the playground. There is a contentment, a placid happiness that still is energetic. There is no attempt to grasp in a few short minutes all the joys of recreation, for no hard and fast time is drawn between work and play. A sense of restfulness and peace and happy work is cultivated, free from anxiety and dread, factors too often present in the school of the old régime."
R. Griffiths: *A Study of Imagination in Early Childhood.*
This was written in 1935!

6. Schools now generally have chairs and tables of suitable height, but mobile furniture of the storage type (shelving or cupboard with wide flat drawers) with which to form 'corners' or 'bays' is also very necessary. The physical act of withdrawal to a special semi-enclosed area greatly helps children's sense of involvement with the work or play in hand, and is a valuable aid to concentration.
7. Chairs and tables should have wooden, not metal legs. If floors are not noise-absorbing, the chair and table-legs need silencers. Expense—minimal.
8. Floors need to be solid, resilient and dirt-resisting, so that children can be bare-footed, or sit, lie and crawl. The cost of adapting and improving all unsuitable floor surfaces would probably be considerable, but should not be shirked.

Apparatus, Books and Equipment

What of the materials with which the Family-grouped class is to work, bearing in mind that "the presence of material is in itself a stimulus to learning"?[1]

They are no different from those found in every good Infants' school, but each room must contain the full range, from that of the Reception class to the most advanced piece of number apparatus or reading book.

As the classroom material for each level of attainment is comparatively small in quantity, its provision is not unduly expensive, especially after the initial outlay is complete, but its organization does call for skill on the part of the teacher (see Chapter 7).

As a general guide to the quality of material which should be available, we have never heard a more succinct comment than the one made by one of Her Majesty's Inspectors who said, "Avoid the trivial."

In the books mentioned below much helpful advice may be found.[2]

A headteacher of a Family-grouped school has given permission to reproduce the notes she gives her own teachers on equipping the infant classroom.

"Creative Work
Sand and Water: objects for playing and experimenting.

---

[1] L. A. Reid: *Philosophy and Education.*
[2] E. Boyce: *The First Year in School.*
   B. Mann: *Learning Through Creative Work.*
   G. Cooper: *The Place of Play in an Infant and Junior School*
   E. Churchill: *Counting and Measuring in the Infants' School.*
   G. Allen and others: *Scientific Interests in the Primary School.*
   N. Goddard: *Reading in the Modern Infants' School.*

Wood: woodwork bench, tool-box, sand paper, assorted nails, rulers, instructions, sawing-boards.

Clay: bins, trays, oilcloth.

Junk Box: various boxes, cotton reels, card, paper, tubes, corrugated cardboard, silver paper, etc.

Building: boxes, bricks, planks, constructional sets.

Sewing, etc.: wools, cottons, buttons, needles, ribbons, etc., peg dolls and pipe-cleaner dolls to dress, patterns, instructions.

Painting: easels, various kinds of paper, paints, cardboard, brushes, crayons, charcoal, pencils (thick and thin).

Puppetry: instructions for making in various ways, cloth, newspaper, paste, wool for hair.

Music Corner: a variety of percussion and melodic instruments, material for making maracas, sticks, drums, B.B.C. pamphlets and other song books.

Dramatic and Imaginative Play

Teacher to equip two home corners as follows:

Bedroom: dolls, dressing table, knitting/sewing drawer, wardrobe with hanging clothes, drawers for underclothes, bed and bedding (covered mattress, underblanket, sheets, blankets, quilts, eiderdown, pillow case), cradle, alarm clock, screens, books of instructions on 'How to make a bed', 'How to tidy our House', and 'Making a Jumper', etc.

Kitchen: dresser, stove, cooking materials, sink unit, dressing-up clothes, instructions, recipe cards.

Writing corner

Children to have free access to paper, paints, crayons, in order that they may draw, paint and write freely. Tins containing thick black pencils, coloured pencils, white and black fat crayons, felt brushes, tracing cards, templates, letter templates, newspaper, kitchen paper, plain paper, writing patterns and copies, alphabet books, picture dictionaries, birthday and pattern books, word books, 'beauty' cards (folders with pictures, etc. and appropriate verse or prose opposite), 'interest' cards (simple reference library).

Suggested Number Equipment

Capacity: deep bath, meat dish, oilcloth and aprons, many pairs of things dissimilar in weight but similar in size (e.g. sponge/stone), three tins of same size (one with hole in bottom, one with several holes half-way up, one with many holes all over), small and large funnels, small bottle with wide neck, large bottle with wide neck, two bottles of different shapes to be filled with same amount of water and a mark to be painted on each bottle, measures, measuring spoons, jug and mug, sand tray with large and small buckets.

Length: measuring box, tape measures, 1-inch cubes (12, 36, 100), analysis of foot, yard sticks, height ladder, height record, ribbons, scissors, work cards, length games, assignment cards.

Weight: balance, spring balance, domestic scales, home-made weights, analysis of weights up to 1 lb., contrasting things to weigh (e.g. beads, ball-bearings, 1-inch and 3-inch nails), natural things to weigh (e.g. chestnuts, cones, pebbles, etc.), dried beans and peas, sand, sawdust, funnel, weighing games, assignment cards.

Sorting, shape-making: bowl with marbles for shapes, patterns and colours, fraction apparatus, floor mosaics, beads, buttons, sticks, shells, assorted shapes in varying sizes.

Counting: skittles (not numbered), Lotto and other games, peg boards, track games, dice, floor dominoes, counters, shells, buttons.

Time: two clocks (one real clock and one toy clock), clock templates and rubber stamp, time lotto game, assignment cards.

Fractions: fraction board, fraction equipment on squares, circles and other shapes, coloured paper, fraction games, assignment cards.

Money: real money for sorting, cards and money for shopping, assignment cards, classroom shop.

This equipment is freely available to children all day, and each teacher has developed her own way of using it."

Summary

The following quotation is taken from Dr. Wall:

"Maturation × Nurture = Development".[1] That is, development depends both upon nature and nurture.

This may at first seem obvious and hardly worth saying, but it carries serious implications for us in school.

How many existing school environments and programmes do justice to the importance of that word 'nurture'?[2] What might a day's work-study of just one child in every classroom in this country reveal? How much boredom, anxiety, indifference to learning? How much time spent waiting for the attention or instruction of a teacher or for other members of the class? How many children are described openly (i.e. in front of them) as 'slow', 'dull', or even 'stupid', because their level of attainment falls below that of their fellows? What incalculable effects upon future personality development do such experiences have? We are only just beginning to discover.

All this must be placed alongside the conscientious efforts of devoted teachers to meet the needs of overlarge classes in inconvenient surroundings, and alongside their brilliant successes too, and those of the children they teach.

But for both teachers and children every available means should be sought to conserve teaching and learning time and energies. Teachers themselves need reassurance when their methods seem to be failing. They also need the kind of school environment in which successful learning is made natural and easy, and in which it is accepted as wiser to wait until children are ready to learn with speed and interest than to exert pressure, either direct or implied, to begin the 'tool' subjects at the earliest possible moment.

What are the characteristics of such a school environment? They are, as stated, those which accept each child at the level *at which he is*, those which harness his own natural curiosity, and those which offer opportunity for developing his full potential.

We cannot dissociate intellectual from emotional and social development; nor, looking upon a child as a person, not merely as a pupil, would we wish to do so. Provision of an environment which caters for all aspects of personality must be made, as far as it is within the limits of our capacity to do so.

Family Grouping, especially where associated with a free approach to learning, seems to us best able to provide such an environment.

---

[1] W. Wall, F. Schonell, W. Olson: *Failure in School.*
[2] "The term 'nurture' is commonly used in the broadest sense to embrace not only feeding but *all* the complexities involved in education and socialization." ibid.

3
Emotional Development

The basis of experience is emotional.[1]
The motive power of learning is the emotional life.[2]

Emotional Development: The Business of Schools

Why need schools be concerned with children's emotional growth? Can this not be left to parents? It is surely the business of schools to concentrate on teaching, or at any rate on learning, and on standards of attainment; not to be concerned with a child's emotions except in so far as it is necessary to train him to control them.

This is an attitude commonly held, not only by parents and the public, but by many teachers also. It is interwoven with the idea that free expression of emotion is not very desirable, and that some emotions in particular are rather shameful. Loving mothers, for instance, will often indignantly deny that an older child is jealous of a younger one, and spiteful expressions by a child of anger or frustration are frequently treated with outraged horror and the child physically punished.

Enlightenment is growing, however, concerning emotional development and the behaviour patterns of children at varying ages. Parents and teachers, with psychological information to guide them, are better able to accept the natural expression of children's feelings, and have greater insight into ways of helping them to satisfactory maturation.

Many teachers have an intuitive insight which serves them well in this respect. Faced with a class of 40 children, they show their awareness of individual temperamental differences by such comments as, "He's rather a baby for his age"; "Such a stable little girl"; "I have to be careful not to upset him"; "Very grown up for her age and rather spoilt"; "Mature and thoughtful, really loves learning"; "Spiteful: takes it out on other children".

Should the school concern itself more than this with emotional growth and maturation?

It should for three reasons:

1. Because a child is one and indivisible. Feeling operates at a deep subconscious level and influences every part of a child's life.

---

[1] A. Whitehead: *The Adventure of Ideas.*
[2] W. Wall: *Education and Mental Health.*

2. Because, accepting that schools have a particular function to perform in directing and encouraging intellectual growth, we must appreciate that the emotional state of a child exerts a profound influence upon his capacity to learn. This is particularly true of the Infants' school years.

3. Because in any person the driving force, or will to learn, is basically an emotional one.

The Wholeness of a Person

The need to think of a child as a whole being is no longer disputed—in theory.

We know that a child's education must be more than Physical Education (for the body), the three Rs (for the mind), the Arts (for the imagination) and Religious Education (for the spirit), and we are often uncomfortably reminded in adult life that success or happiness depends more on what a person is like than on what he can do. Dr. Hughes[1] forcefully reminds us that there are more ways than one of being backward. The clumsy person is backward in muscular skill, the gauche or aggressive are socially backward and the aesthetically retarded, though sometimes intelligent, are backward in feeling. We meet such people in adult life. Could education have helped them more had there been a better understanding of their needs?

The whole is more than just the sum of the parts. M. L. Jacks, discussing this, suggests that the answer to the sum, "if sum there be", may perhaps be found in "the total combination of relationships between these parts, and not in the mere addition of the parts themselves".[2]

But perhaps Gesell expresses this totality most simply and most succinctly by saying of a child ". . . if we take him apart he vanishes; he ceases to be a person".[3] And quoting from Dr. Wall: "The emotional life of a child is a vital and indivisible part—perhaps even the most important part of him."[4]

In the last chapter we suggested that Infants' teachers aspire to give opportunity for the best growth to every child. Such growth must include emotional growth; emotional factors pervade every aspect of a child's personal structure and no Infants' teacher can do her job properly without understanding this.

Intuition and experience are useful guides, and many a child has

---

[1] A. Hughes: *Education and the Democratic Ideal.*

[2] M. Jacks: *Total Education.*

[3] A. Gesell and F. Ilg: *The Child from Five to Ten.*

[4] W. Wall, F. Schonell, W. Olson: *Failure in School*; speaking of conditions which influence learning, and changes in the pattern of the field at the time of learning the authors say, "Of the various kinds of field, by far the most important is the emotional."

been helped through emotional disturbances by teachers relying upon them. But teachers themselves are frequently anxious about manifestations of strong feeling in children. They are not sure how permissive to be in the face of aggression or destructiveness, or what outlets for feeling should be provided in a classroom, especially one primarily geared to academic work. Faced with a timid or uncooperative learner, they are not sure how much pressure it is proper to exert upon him.

Expert Help: Emotional Maturation

Teachers need no longer rely solely upon intuition and experience. "The demonstration of the close interdependence and interaction of these aspects of personality (intellectual, social and emotional) is perhaps the major contribution which the biological and dynamic psychologists have made to education."[1] Many studies[2] of child psychology describe the modes of thinking and behaviour normal for children at varying ages. No teacher or parent need be anxious when the 5-year-old, self-contained but self-centred, plays alone, or finds difficulty in fitting into group activities. But the 7-year-old who withdraws into isolation causes concern for the satisfactory development of his mental health. Similarly a stable 5-year-old who regresses at 6 to outbursts of temper or aggression reminiscent of a toddler can be accepted philosophically, and handled objectively in the knowledge that this is a normal element in emotional growth. Manifested in a Junior child, however, it may well be regarded more seriously.

This is not to suggest that an Infants' teacher plays the part of a passive, uninvolved onlooker. If she is aware of the nature and pattern of emotional growth, her daily programmed curriculum *and her attitudes* will allow for its proper manifestation. Indeed, such provision will be regarded as of equal importance with fresh air, good food and good books.

"Emotions are not independent forces which in some mysterious way take possession of the child. They are structured modes of reaction which yield to the organizing influence of experience and education."[3] Exactly what *influences* and *experiences* must schools provide to ensure satisfactory emotional maturation?

The answer is the same as that for all growth. Situations must be arranged which encourage the optimum development of emotional maturity, recognize individual differences and try to satisfy needs as

---

[1] W. Wall: *Education and Mental Health.*
[2] A. Gesell and F. Ilg: *The Child from Five to Ten.*
   S. Isaacs: *Intellectual Growth in Young Children.*
   A. Bowley: *The Natural Development of the Child.*
[3] A. Gesell and F. Ilg: *The Child from Five to Ten.*

they arise. As far as conditions permit, schools must understand and accept emotional immaturity as it manifests itself, and make available the means by which children can stabilize satisfactory patterns of behaviour at the time most appropriate.

"When children are born, they know nothing: later learning depends on the quantity and quality of their play."[1] We should not press too early the attainment of academic skills, for we know that, "by seven years a child has usually worked his way through earlier difficulties, and approaches what is known as the latency period, in which emotional aspects of development are less pronounced . . . energies are set free for more definite intellectual work, and more advanced active pursuits."[2]

We should have some appreciation of what these *earlier difficulties* are, and know that there is a significant difference between not pressing the three Rs upon children, and not making such skills available to those who show spontaneous interest in them.

Of course teachers have always been aware of differences in children's temperaments and have been willing to allow for them, but as we have said, they are sometimes uneasy about how much individuality to tolerate, or how best to help individuals to 'grow up'. At the same time they themselves feel the pressure and a sense of urgency about 'getting them on' or anxiety about time lost in 'pandering' to individual temperamental difficulties.

Peel, speaking of widely differing temperamental, emotional and physical qualities in individual children, says, "It does not need a psychologist to remind the teacher of this variation, but it is strange that many teachers require to be reminded of its educational consequences. Most teachers recognize intellectual variety but many fail to take sufficient account of the emotional and temperamental differences of their pupils."[3]

The help of the expert in explaining the nature of individual differences and the behavioural and emotional patterns of the maturing child may be easily found. Research and study supply the facts and psychologists communicate them. But to the teacher falls the task of carrying them into practice. It is hardly surprising that we do not always succeed.

Dr. Bowley lists the characteristics of the pre-school child which appear to her to be "indicative of satisfactory emotional development".[4] They are printed on the left-hand side of the next page and contrasted on the right with their opposites.

---

[1] M. Brearley: TV programme, 1964.
[2] R. Griffiths: *A Study of Imagination in Early Childhood.*
[3] A. Peel: *The Psychological Basis of Education.*
[4] A Bowley: *The Natural Development of the Child.*

DR. BOWLEY'S LIST	OPPOSITES
To appear contented and serene	To appear anxious or tense
To show affection naturally	To be shy, withdrawn or unduly reserved
To be able to tolerate restrictions	To be impatient, rebellious or recalcitrant
To appear keen and alert, and alive to new experiences	To seem dull, lazy and indifferent to new experiences
To show a certain degree of independence, and to attempt to handle difficulties alone	To appear over-dependent, unwilling or unable to make self-initiated effort

Dr. Bowley refers to a child *before* he starts school. Yet Infants' classes are full of children evincing the characteristics listed on the right. Often children arrive at school exhibiting one or more of them. Only too frequently they are still there, or have even been developed when the children pass into the Junior school.

Bearing in mind that, "the Primary school years are the period of transition, development and organization, not only in the intellectual life but in the social and emotional growth of children,"[1] it is imperative that provision be made for this transition, development and organization, and that children's personalities are not stultified by lack of suitable conditions in which to grow.

Maturation cannot be by-passed. In fact children who have been deprived of opportunities to pass through normal stages of growth will instinctively seize a chance to regress if it is presented to them.

The picture facing page 48 shows a 7-year-old boy from a poor, overcrowded home who transferred, by the chance of removal, from a formal school where he was failing academically to a freer Family-grouped one. He was silent and anxious, and was further handicapped in social relationships because his English was far from fluent. For a long time he played alone at very simple pursuits like a 5-year-old, with an intensity and concentration which clearly showed his need. In due course he discarded this stage of play, never to return to it. His tension and reticence was replaced by an infectious cheerfulness and he became a popular, sociable member of the older group. His tool subjects also improved. No doubt many teachers could cite such examples of children maturing naturally at their own rate, given suitable opportunities.

The Importance of Play
    It is fortunate for the teacher that play is such a supremely valuable

---

[1] W. Wall: *Education and Mental Health.*

vehicle for growth. If the school makes available many varied types of play, most individual emotional needs and temperamental difficulties can be catered for. Through the manipulation of symbols in play, through dramatic and other self-expression, and by using each other, often to supply mutually compatible needs, children will grow to levels of emotional stability which it is hardly possible for them to attain without such opportunities.

Wheeler, writing of the cathartic function of free play, underlines its vital importance by saying, "Play is the supreme psychological need of the young child: a satisfaction necessary for mental health," and asks this arresting question—"What man is there of you, whom if his son ask bread will he give him a stone, or if he ask a fish, will he give him a serpent, or if he ask to play, will he give him the three Rs?"[1]

This question was asked in 1939. Infants' schools exist where even yet the staple diet is that of the three Rs, and little else. This is not through lack of concern for children's welfare, but through lack of understanding. Intellectual needs cannot be filled *before* those of emotional and social growth, but are dependent upon and grow out of full satisfaction of them. Play is often the means of such growth. Moreover, in the mind of a child, the division between play and work is blurred until it becomes non-existent; satisfaction and purpose generated in the one transfer imperceptibly to the other.

This does not happen by accident though. Hard thinking and careful planning go into preparation for children's play. Experience and conviction alleviate teachers' anxieties about the 'time-wasting' aspects of play, for teachers begin to look with new eyes and see for themselves that play is indeed 'spontaneous self-instruction'.

This is only, of course, if the material and situations available for the children are truly satisfying at all levels and in all areas of development. Most Infants' schools allow children to play some of the time. Time-table concessions vary; they include the leisurely Free-Day programme described in Chapter 2, or free play for an hour each morning, a period often described as 'activity' (are other periods of the day to be thought of as 'passivity'?)—or about three-quarters of an hour once or twice a week. At the extreme end of the play spectrum it is an hour on Friday afternoons when children bring their own toys and are allowed to play with them.

Clearly there are widely different estimates of the value and purpose of play for the Infant. Here is a view given by Dr. Ruth Griffiths: "The child needs all his energy, so great is the task that life has set him; during these early years he has comparatively more to accomplish than at any later similar period. Play, fantasy, and day-dreaming are his instruments and into these channels his energy flows. Any system of

---

[1] O. Wheeler and I. Earl: *Nursery School Education.*

education that hampers this natural direction of energy endangers the health, mental or physical, of the child. Play is no mere extraneous activity in children, it is the business of life. Any system of education that is to be effective must utilize the play activity of the child."[1]

Another view is given by Bowley: "In play the child not only overcomes painful reality, but is assisted in mastering his instinctive fear and internal dangers by projecting them into the outer world. So a child gains emotional relief in the most natural and simple way possible."[2]

How often shall a child play in school? When he needs to. And for how long? For as long as he needs to.

Won't he play all the time?

Not if the provision for emotional development is satisfying, and that for intellectual development easily accessible and inviting.

An enormously wide range of material is needed, but once provided, is easily maintained. A list has already been given on pages 37–8 of Chapter 2 and the reader is further referred to H. Stone: *Some Play Materials for Children Under Eight*, which not only gives a comprehensive list of suitable materials but also hints on their care and use.

The more varied and challenging the material (though not necessarily the more expensive) the more emotionally and intellectually satisfying the play will be. Inadequate play material in poor condition—dirty, broken, too small or insufficiently challenging—leads to quarrelling, aggression and frustration. It is better for the children that they have teacher-directed lessons instead.

Reception-class teachers are used to providing and caring for play equipment and think nothing of it. Teachers used to a Family-grouped class testify that many older children show the need for play materials traditionally associated with younger children. This may be surprising at first. *All* children seem to need *all* the material at some time or another. The idea that children have grown away from 'sand and water' by the time they are ready to leave the Reception class must be abandoned, because it is not true in practice. There is of course more than one way to play with sand and water.[3]

---

[1] R. Griffiths: *A Study of Imagination in Early Childhood.*

[2] A. Bowley: *The Natural Development of the Child* (quoting Klein: *The Psycho-Analysis of Childhood*).

[3] The writer saw a group of 7-year-old children working on some advanced water-play discovery. They set a number of wooden boxes one upon the other beside the water tray, and arranged a jar of water at a height, with funnel and tubes carrying the water to a lower level. It was controlled by pinching the tube. They tried to transfer the water *up* the tube from the lower to the higher levels. At this point a teacher could well join in such investigation and draw attention to the behaviour of water and point out the similar functions of a tap and the fingers pinching the tube.

S. Isaacs describes investigations begun in this way and leading to the understanding of cisterns, pipes, valves and pumps.

This is particularly true of children living in restrictive environments—high blocks of flats, houses without gardens, overcrowded rooms—or of those who spend much of their spare time in passive activities such as watching TV or riding in cars.

Some children show distinct preferences for certain items of equipment—big blocks for example, or painting. But it does not follow that such children will be of the same approximate age. In brick play there may be an older boy directing and organizing the play while younger ones join in. The 'baby' in home play is not always one of the younger children; some older ones like to be mothered, while a young one may take the opportunity to be a figure of power and authority, playing out a situation in which in life he or she is the most helpless.

The special value of play in Family-grouped classes is that *children of uneven development find the level which suits them best*: the young clever child can choose older playmates for the stimulation of his intellect, or a younger kind of play for his emotional need. The slow learner, possibly at a disadvantage even in a play situation with more able children of his own age, finds a value status in the eyes of younger members of the class for his greater organizing ability or social aptitude.

He can fetch materials, organize and control them better and clear them away more efficiently. He can teach a game and be a stable focus or leader for a younger group who might otherwise quarrel among themselves. "Emotional satisfaction compensates for intellectual inadequacies and contentment carries over into intellectual effort . . . emotional processes pervade all his life, private and social, genial and elevating, as well as violent and disturbing."[1]

Classroom Atmosphere

Apart from accelerating physical growth, stimulating mental development and facilitating emotional stability, the wholesome effect which satisfactory free play has upon the atmosphere of the classroom is most marked. A sentiment of good humour develops between class-mates and towards the teacher. Emphasis is on co-operation rather than competition. The more pleasurable feelings—contentment, enthusiasm, affection, tenderness, humour, serenity—are accentuated and where these positive attitudes exist there is a good chance they will displace ill-temper, jealousy and sulkiness.

Gesell appeals for more humour in the classroom (observing somewhat wrily that "it is not an official subject"), and comments on the wholesome effect it has on personality development, and the lack of it in some children, especially at six years—the age of emotional tension and ferment. He points out that it does not consist of being 'funny' but

---

[1] A. Gesell and F. Ilg: *The Child from Five to Ten.*

in an attitude of affability and cheerful give-and-take which spreads *by contagion.*[1]

Adjusting: Problem Solving: Fantasy Play

The subject of play and a child's emotional life must include reference to the enormous importance of fantasy play.

This is found in all sorts of imaginings. In home play, dressing up, being the adult in a hundred different situations . . . mother, father, baby, doctor, nurse, driver, teacher, spaceman . . . the list is endless. In drawing, painting and creative work (children seem to have an almost compulsive need to draw—see Chapter 5), in symbolic play with sand, water, clay, vehicles and other toys, and in day-dreaming, it pervades and invades children's free lives and given proper scope is the medium above all others by which a child ingests experience, adjusts to an ever-growing compass of relationships, and handles the intellectual problems and emotional dilemmas which arise from these.

Despite the insight into the structure and functioning of our mental lives which psychologists have given us, there are still many people to whom the idea of children's 'problems' (apart from the obvious ones of physical neglect, ill-treatment or misfortune) is unreal and the concept of a child's fantasy life is unwelcome. Children play to 'let off steam' or 'use surplus energy' and day-dreaming may be thought 'unhealthy'—certainly no part of the life of a sturdy, normal child. To such adults, childhood is still, "the happiest years of your life".

Perceptive adults, on the other hand, know better. From babyhood to the onset of latency (7 to 8 years) a child's existence is one of continuous adaption and reorientation. His world expands bewilderingly fast; knowledge and new relationships increase in number and complexity. Play affords the opportunity to mull over ideas, to recapitulate experience, and to distinguish between the real and the imaginary.

"Between five and seven years a child can frequently be seen confusing fantasy with reality in his play. Thereafter he becomes more of a realist, though fantasy will continue."[2]

Distinguishing between the subjective and the objective world is not a child's only difficulty though. Emotions stirred by the very fact of being a child and being at the mercy of adult whims and requirements, or fears and anxieties arising from half-knowledge, ignorance and inadequacy, can all be discharged through play. Negative and positive feelings for others can be expressed without fear of the consequences or feelings of guilt.

McFarland compares an adult's way of dealing with a situation which has disturbed him with that of a child: "Adults, by their

---

[1] A. Gesell and F. Ilg: *The Child from Five to Ten.*
[2] K. Lovell: *Educational Psychology and Children.*

A 7-year-old at solitary play (see page 44)

A handicap is being overcome (see page 57)

greater emotional and linguistic maturity, are able to discuss their personal problems with others, or are able to reflect upon them analytically. Children are poorly equipped to work out their personal problems at an intellectual level. Their play represents a reflection upon the world and themselves."[1]

He refers to the relief which children find in play when pressured by some problem, and speaks of "a discharge of pent-up emotion. Play is both diagnostic and therapeutic".

This purging is referred to also by Erikson,[2] who points out that a traumatic experience "triggers off more excitement than can be managed". For an adult, talk, and for a child, play, provides the means of releasing this excitement. Teachers' experiences of children at play have made them familiar with the need to act out domestic, school or other situations which have aroused strong feelings. Books of child study and educational method are full of descriptions of such cathartic play.

Simpson and Alderson have some particularly good examples. Their Chapter VIII, "Children with Problems and Difficulties", opens with the remark: "A child's choice of activity often indicates the nature of his problem and the kind of play he chooses often helps to relieve that problem."[3] Investigation shows the frequency of the following problems:

Feelings of insecurity (temporary or permanent).
Over-indulgence, producing waywardness and uncertainty.
Inability to concentrate for various reasons.
Aggression or destructiveness (indications of a need for power and a sense of inadequacy).
Fears or guilt feelings inducing an unnatural tidiness and an objection to handling messy materials.

Simpson and Alderson consider that the 'effortless' child has the most intractable problem to solve: it is significant that he is often, "an intelligent child who has had the academic side overdeveloped at too early an age". Reference is also made to the "gifted child of high intelligence who seems unable to make any creative effort". In their book the play of such children is discussed with insight; records extending over several weeks are quoted and details given of the ways in which difficulties are handled. Books of child psychology discuss children's problems, but not always with such sensitivity.

Investigation at a greater depth is made by Ruth Griffiths[4] and all the difficulties are discussed together with:

[1] H. McFarland: *Psychology and Teaching*.
[2] E. Erikson: *Discussion on Child Development*.
[3] D. Simpson and D. Alderson: *Creative Play in the Infants' School*.
[4] R. Griffiths: *A Study of Imagination in Early Childhood*.

D

Intellectual problems described as closely interrelated with emotional ones—"the one growing out of the other, as well as reacting the one upon the other".

Fear of failure in school. A case of this kind is cited in a 5-year-old with an IQ of 129!

Fear of disasters. (Very prevalent in young, intelligent children. The fearful child compensates by being courageous in his fantasy life: fears are overcome by 'working over' the feared things, e.g. in stories of horses, dogs or fire.)

Inferior feelings. (Evidence of the small, weak personality striving against the repressions of the environment.)

It should be clearly understood that although some children have exceptional problems and difficulties, *all* children have some of these problems some of the time. Much of a child's mental and emotional life is inaccessible to us; we have little recollection of what it is like to be 5, 6 or 7 years old, except for the few incidents which have impressed themselves upon our memory (all of which have strong emotional overtones). Children cannot tell us, except by their behaviour and actions, but we can exercise imagination and have some conception, for instance, of their feelings of inadequacy in an adult world, and appreciate how far beyond the bounds of realization are some of their wishes.

Speaking of their fantasy goals Erikson says, "What a child wants to get at, to go to, to see, to touch and to understand—their selection of these goals and persistence in approaching them vastly outdoes children's ability to master these goals . . . they are transferred to the area of play."[1]

Through imagination, we may have some idea of the satisfaction and relief from frustration which children can be afforded simply by giving them opportunity for freely-chosen imaginative activity. We see the release of feelings stirred in them about people or against authority in the aggressive 'cops and robbers' type of play, or in drawings filled with bombing planes and warships. We also note a chance to inflict punishment on others, or fears faced when children pretend to be fierce or perform hazardous feats. Expressions of aggressive tendencies are "accompanied by a vast abreaction of pent-up emotion, and the restoring of equilibrium with healthy, positive emotional accompaniment".[2]

We are not so easily able to understand play manifestations of pure fantasy, through which, the depth psychologists tell us, fears may be rationalized and feelings of guilt and anger mastered. In her revealing book, Dr. Griffiths presents evidence of children's imagination at work over a period of weeks in drawing, dreams, language and blot

[1] E. Erikson: *Discussions on Child Development.*
[2] R. Griffiths: *A Study of Imagination in Early Childhood.*

tests. She explains that "until a vague emotion is symbolized in some objective way (depicted or discussed) it is impossible for a child to overcome it". And she makes it clear that "a child comes gradually to find ways to overcome or destroy the enemy. Step by step, he makes his problem explicit and tends to find a solution."[1]

Four points of considerable significance for the teacher of young children emerge from a study of Ruth Griffiths's book. Firstly, there is no need for the teacher to be a psycho analyst: the teacher does nothing but provide opportunities for imaginative activity. Secondly, we can never know through what medium a child's subconscious will find a solution for his difficulties; we must supply all we can and leave the choice to him.

Thirdly, the persistence shown by children in constantly selecting the same medium reflects their need of it. Whilst making sure that they appreciate all the possibilities available we should be slow to divert a child from any particular piece of equipment or type of material which is obviously giving him satisfaction. We must particularly beware of yielding to the feeling that "It's time he gave that up now," or of making derogatory comments such as, "That's rather a babyish toy for you, isn't it?"

Fourthly, we note that children may not engage continuously on their own problem-solving. There is no suggestion that children, even at Infants' level, need to be constantly engaged in play, or free-choice activities.

Problem-solving at subconscious level is a constant human activity, as J. A. Hadfield's *Dreams and Nightmares* makes plain. But it is only part of life, though it probably uses a far larger part of a child's mental energy than we have supposed. Opportunity must be there: it must be freely available along with proper conditions for physical health and provision for mental growth.

It is the teacher's skill which keeps the mixture right: fortunately children themselves are impelled to select what they need at the appropriate time; unconsciously chosen play will relieve feelings of which they are unaware at conscious level.

"The psycho-analysis of young children by Klein's play technique has shown that engines and motors, fires and lights, water and mud and animals have a profoundly symbolic meaning for them, rooted in infantile fantasy."[2]

A teacher need not be a psychologist, but she needs to be aware of the satisfactions, consolations and emotional motivations which operate on choices of material for free play, and see that there is plenty available.

---

[1] R. Griffiths: *A Study of Imagination in Early Childhood.*
[2] S. Isaacs: *Intellectual Growth in Young Children.*

Ruth Griffiths makes this clear in her summary of the functions of childhood fantasy:

1. Fantasy or imagination provides the normal means for the solution of development problems in young children.

2. The problem is attacked indirectly, is often disguised by symbolism, and the subject is only vaguely aware of the end towards which he is striving.

3. The problem develops by means of a series of successively imagined solutions, which constitute a piecemeal and gradual resolution of the problem.

4. The result of the process is found both in an acquisition of information by the subject, and also in the more prominent feature of a change of mental attitude.

5. The change of attitude is usually from a personal and subjective point of view to a more socialized and objective one.

Dr. Griffiths concludes by recommending "a type of education which, while checking unsocial attitudes at conscious level, gives ample opportunity for the free expression of fantasy, and scope for play activities."[1]

Play Groups in the Family-grouped Classroom

What advantages for play are there in Family-grouped classrooms which cannot equally well be supplied by the more customary Horizontal Age-grouping? Many schools provide such opportunities but it seems more likely that needs at all levels can be supplied in a room equipped for children of 5 to 7 years.

Children can regress to an earlier stage of play without remark, and the teacher is less likely to be made anxious by such regression because she sees each child's development over a longer period and knows him better. Moreover, there is a naturalness about the play-groups which form, break up and form again, reflecting the composition of a family at home. These groups have the same constitution as those which form spontaneously in the street, composed of children from toddler-age to the fringe of the single-sex groups of the 8 to 10-year-old girls and boys.

Emotional make-up varies from child to child, and in the same children from day to day. So far from being a source of difficulty to the teacher, this fact makes her task easier.

The 5-year-old is an egocentric little person, concerned mainly with himself, his mother, his home and with his immediate adjustment to school: forty 5-year-olds are an almost impossible task for one teacher.

"Starting school is for the child a second weaning process.... It is often on going to school that the child first learns that his experiences

---

[1] R. Griffiths: *A Study of Imagination in Early Childhood.*

do not necessarily coincide with those of his mother. He learns that things may happen to him and thoughts and feelings arise in him of which she can have no knowledge unless he reports them. Lacking powers of expression and not realizing the necessity for giving the background of his story, he finds that his mother does not enter into his experience. This is new and strange and may be frightening to him. It may bring his first fully conscious realization that he is, in a sense, isolated."[1]

Although there is no substitute for his mother—and this is a factor in the adjustment required of him—the 5-year-old is not isolated in a Family-grouped class. There is an anchor in the class—an evident link with home. Much of the confidence and help he needs—some of it in comparatively trivial matters—can be given by an older child, perhaps unconsciously, by example.

The 6-year-old is going through an unsettled period of physical and emotional growth. He is often restless, lively and difficult to manage. Forty 6-year-olds can present a considerable problem. Many remain immature, recalcitrant and dissatisfied with school life well into their seventh year. Twelve are more easily accommodated than forty.

The 7-year-olds can manage long periods of purposeful self-initiated effort with occasional direction from the adult. Their stability and leadership can present a behaviour goal to younger children. Responsibility develops personality, but in many a classroom of forty 'top' infants it is only the most mature or intelligent who can be given responsible tasks. Turn and turn-about is the best that can be managed. It is much easier to give a true measure of responsibility to older children in the Family-grouped class. Both in play and work, 7-year-olds evince the intellectual progress of children ending their Infants' school life.

"As the child emerges successfully from this period (5 to 7 years) . . . energy tends to be set free for more objective and more strictly intellectual tasks, the satisfactory approach to which will depend very largely upon the way in which the child has been able to resolve the earlier emotional problems."[1]

Other Outlets for Emotion: Writing

Brief reference only will be made to the outlets and stimuli for emotion and imagination which are commonly accepted in schools, such as painting and craft work, drama, music and movement, poetry and stories (see Chapter 6).

No teacher needs reminding of the emotional satisfaction found in

---

[1] H. James and others: *Periods of Stress in the Primary School.*
[2] R. Griffiths: *A Study of Imagination in Early Childhood.*

intellectual achievement, and further reference will be made later in this chapter to some aspects of this.

A particularly important medium of expression for some children is language, either written or spoken. There is new awareness of the value of fantasy-release and the handling of disturbing emotion through language.

Where free creative writing in its various forms is encouraged (see Chapter 5) teachers often become aware that the outpouring of emotion has released tension or that some disturbing situation has been resolved.

To illustrate this point, we print a story taken from a collection freely written by a 7-year-old girl of bright personality and good intelligence. Her writing makes frequent reference to mildly frightening situations, reflecting anxiety about animals and powerful people.

THE LITTLE GIRL WHO WENT TO SCHOOL

"One day there lived a little girl and her name was Nicola, and Nicola did not comb her hair when she went to school and she did not clean her teeth and she did not wash and when she got to school her teacher said why did you not brush your hair and you did not brush your teeth, and Nicola was sced X scead when her teacher told her off. And her teacher give her some work to, and Nicola ccried and her teacher said why are you cria x crying and Nicola said I am crying because I can not do this work and her teacher said that is not a thing to cry about and Nicola was 8 years old and she could not cont count up to 100 and in 10s so her teacher told her and when Nicola came back to school agian she had did her hair and washed."

Later Growth

With the ultimate development of children in mind, it should not be forgotten that emotional problems unresolved in the early years, and sinking back from prominence during the latency period, tend to reemerge in adolescence. Satisfactory emotional maturation in the Infants' school years helps to establish mental health for life. We cannot, of course, entirely eliminate stress or unhappiness from a child's life, nor would we wish to do so, but we can and should provide environmental opportunities for working through difficulties, adjusting and coming to terms with them. By these means personality is strengthened, a child gains in stature and takes positive steps towards increasing his mental health.

"Stress is inherent in living: reaction to stress is a factor in the maintenance of health: the manner of reaction is an index of the quality of health . . . the pattern of reaction laid down in childhood tends to persist throughout life."[1]

---

[1] H. James and others: *Periods of Stress in the Primary School.*

The child who has the opportunity to take vigorous steps towards solving his problems through subconscious symbolization or imaginative play is more likely to establish a pattern of positive mental health than one who, overcome or withdrawn, is unable to deal with either the real situation or the psychic one.

Basic personality patterns will be a major factor in determining the energy with which difficulties are tackled, even symbolically, but so too will environmental opportunity.

"We believe" says a study made by the National Association for Mental Health, "that present-day school life involves considerable strain, especially at certain periods: some of this is unnecessary and may be eliminated; some is inevitable and must be faced".[1] Amongst these stresses particular mention is made of entry into school and of transition.

Instead of helping children forward, transition often "cuts across their development, checks progress and causes regression and warping. For example, transfer from Infants' to Junior school in this country at the age of 7 years comes too early for many children."[2] Little is said of transfer from class to class within the Infants' school, but "the effects of too-early transition are seen in an increase of both emotional problems such as nail-biting, enuresis, fear of school, spitefulness, and of learning difficulties, for example a standstill in reading, free writing and number."[3]

Teachers and parents can testify to the appearance of many such stress symptoms in children as they pass from class to class.

The responsibility for establishing a pattern of healthy emotional development in the early school years is heavy. Infants' teachers must help to bear it.

Looking with grave concern at present-day adult society's tension, nervous disorders, emotional conflicts, mental illness, crime rates and moral disturbances, we could wish to turn back the clock and look at these people as Infants in the schoolroom, seeking from the start some possible explanation. This we cannot do, but research may presently aid us.[4] Meanwhile we can pay heed to the following:

"Just as one finds in children that inability to play is a serious symptom of emotional disturbance and regression, so one finds that the damming up of creative expression in adolescence and its practical absence from the lives of many adults is at once an effect and the cause of many of the psychological ills from which individuals and society

---

[1] ibid.
[2] ibid.
[3] ibid.
[4] A chair of criminology has recently been established at Cambridge University.

appear to be suffering."[1] We must provide the opportunities children need.

It is no use saying, "The task of the schools is to teach. Achieve the skills and then use them in creative activity." We must accept, and cultivate in others less aware, an attitude that the means of expression (art, languages, mathematical symbols or music) are servants, not masters. They developed historically as channels of communication, because their exponents had something to say. For children they are interwoven with need and satisfaction: there is in them a purpose that is felt in the child.

Educationalists, of course, have been saying this for a very long time. Overcrowded classrooms, the human inadequacies of teachers faced with too many pupils, and similar difficulties, have slowed down the realization of ideals, but the children can help themselves if only they are allowed to do so.

Children with Special Difficulties

The foregoing remarks are generally applicable to all children. There are some with special difficulties who can be greatly helped by the stability of the Family-grouped class, the opportunity to remain for a long time with the same teacher, and the close liaison that can develop between a mother and a teacher who has more than one child successively with her.

A physically handicapped child or one with a speech or hearing defect will obviously benefit by staying with a teacher who knows and understands him. The effort of adjusting to a new teacher, a new classroom or new companions is even more difficult for such a child. Some Traditionally-grouped schools have dealt with such problems by leaving a child 'down' with the same teacher, but this can produce feelings of inferiority or anxiety.

The writers have had experience of two totally deaf children in Family-grouped classes, who, with hearing aids, the confidence inspired by long-standing familiarity with their teacher, consideration and help given by known companions, and the expert help of the appropriate clinic, mastered their handicaps and could read and communicate with other children in the class in a remarkable way. The sight of a deaf child joining with hearing children in creative music-making, with a drum clasped tightly to his chest; and the moving picture of the hearing children who, quickly grasping the technique, turned the deaf child's face towards them so that he might lip-read, will not be forgotten. Several local authorities have groups of children with defective hearing within the organization of Family-grouped schools. The children spend part of their time receiving special help

---

[1] W. Wall: *Education and Mental Health.*

with a trained teacher and equipment for the deaf, and part of every day with their own Family-grouped class.

The photograph facing page 49 illustrates a story of a child with a very severe speech handicap, following an accident in earlier life. The happy-looking little boy leading the line to the slide is almost a year older than anyone else in the group. Admitted to the school at $3\frac{1}{2}$ years for special reasons, distressed and totally without speech, it took him four years to adjust, to enjoy school and to begin to talk. Almost all this advance was made through play in a Family-grouped class, where there were always companions to suit his need and who, in turn, found him a satisfactory playmate. He has now developed sufficient confidence to receive help at a speech clinic.

Dr. Wall refers to, "The very shy boy or girl who gives no overt trouble, (who) often suffers severely in his first class. He is likely to remain mute, to join in no activities, and his very shyness may mask his real ability. Teachers sometimes regard such children as dull, or lazy, and other children tease them."[1]

He further suggests, "The Reception class teacher should never ask such shy children questions they cannot answer, but should try to engage them in some small activity, and praise them privately for any progress they make. Other children may be asked, discreetly, and obliquely, to help."

In a Family-grouped classroom there will be no need to ask. Other children will naturally help. And there is every chance that 2 to 3 years with the same teacher will establish full confidence and allow for the development of all intellectual capacities.

The records of teachers in Family-grouped classes could tell of many maladjusted children finding security and ease through its particular advantages. The writers have chosen only one, to illustrate the special way in which Family-grouping helped.

Sandra was a child of above average intelligence who joined a Family-grouped class at the beginning of her second year in the Infants' school at the age of six. Her mother had been under treatment for depression both as an in-patient and an out-patient of mental hospitals. Because of her emotional instability her mother was unable to make satisfactory relationships with neighbours and had isolated herself, being convinced that everyone was against her. She has an obsession about cleanliness and the welfare of her children, and was overprotective towards them.

When Sandra first entered the Family-grouped class the mother frequently burst into the classroom to make complaints, or to say that the child was sick and could not attend. Often the implication was that the teacher disliked Sandra, and made school so unpleasant for

---

[1] W. Wall: *Education and Mental Health.*

her that she was very unhappy and hated school so much that she was sick through anxiety in the morning. The child was certainly anxious, but it seemed likely the anxiety arose in the home, and that school was providing relief for her. It also seemed likely that the mother's possessive attitude made it difficult for her to tolerate the fact that Sandra could be happy away from her.

Sandra could not sit or stand still even for a few minutes; her face always showed tension. Inability to concentrate made progress in the basic skills extremely slow. She had no real friends of her own age, as like her mother, she was unable to establish good social relationships and was constantly quarrelling.

It was noticeable that in the Family-grouped class she nearly always looked for her friends among children younger than herself. During her third year in the Infants' school (second in the Family-grouped class) she was seldom with children of her own age, but played happily with children two years younger than herself. When asked about her special friends she gave only the names of younger children, her main friends being two particularly immature 5-year-olds. With these she enjoyed playing with sand, water, clay and paint, obviously gaining satisfaction from activities at the level of the 5-year-old. Much of her time was spent in the 'home corner'. When asked whether she liked being mother to the little children she replied that she liked being 'baby' best. Sandra said she did not want to go up into the Juniors because she would miss the little children and did not like playing with the older ones. Mothers of younger children told her mother how she had taken their little children under her wing and taken great care of them in school.

In normal circumstances we should not wish to see a child associating to such a large extent with children so much younger, but in this case it was clear that a much-needed opportunity for regression to more babyish activities was being provided. This could not have been done so easily in an age-grouped class without Sandra becoming conspicuous. Without the younger children, she would probably have become very solitary and would have been unable to obtain such satisfaction through play. Certainly she would not have had such opportunity for social adjustment.

By the age of $7\frac{1}{2}$ Sandra was much happier in school and had to some extent come to terms with her very difficult home circumstances. Although her attainments were still below what would normally be expected from a child of her intelligence she was making reasonable progress and was finding a great deal of satisfaction in her work. She became enthusiastic about school and made a positive contribution to class activities. This resulted in better relationships with the other children and much more cooperation between home and school.

The Failing Child

What of the 'lazy' child; the dull; the backward; the retarded—in short, the child who is failing—the child who in a normal class of 6 or 7-year-olds is found in the 'tail'?

The Family Grouping situation has something very special to offer the emotional health of such a child.

"Failure to learn nearly always has emotional connotations . . . not infrequently retardation is a symptom of adverse attitudes, habits and maladjustments in the entire social and emotional development of the child, which find their roots in experiences in the family and in the early years at school."[1]

Teachers know a great deal about this. They speak regretfully of having to send up children before they are ready to go. They realize that the work a child is required to do is frequently unsuitable for him and he can only manage it with difficulty; or that he needs more help than there is time to give him. They see clear evidence of lowered morale in dislike of school or certain tasks, or in carelessly performed work: they are aware of the emotional stress. But, caught up in the day-to-day routine and pressures there often seems little they can do about it and the child may be blamed for lack of effort.

Family Grouping cannot cure the difficulties a child has to face; nor should all obstacles be removed fom the childhood path, but it does give opportunity for easy regression to an earlier stage of learning, for freely chosen play or symbolic creativeness, for unselfconscious practice at appropriate intellectual levels, and above all for the insight and knowledge a teacher develops in handling the same child for prolonged periods, which makes it possible for her quickly to seize on starting points for learning or calmly accept regression in work or behaviour.

All these assets may not be exclusive to Family Grouping, but they can certainly be achieved more easily within its framework. The emotional element in the failure of the failing child may have, as suggested earlier in this chapter, one of two aspects, or possibly both. Emotional disturbances may cause retardation by interfering with mental growth. It cannot be said too often that "learning in the strictly educational sense will not proceed satisfactorily if the child's emotional life is disturbed."[2] All authorities agree on the adverse effect of emotional disturbances on learning. For example: "Anxiety is highly unfavourable to free inquiry and interest in the objective world," says Susan Isaacs, who gives striking examples to back up her statement.[3] Most teachers could give their own, and would agree that,

---

[1] W. Wall: *Education and Mental Health.*
[2] ibid.
[3] S. Isaacs: *Intellectual Growth in Young Children.*

"mental alertness and an active interest in objects are very dependent upon freedom from anxiety and inner tension".

Disturbance in emotional and social growth is often directly linked with intellectual failure in school . . . "the two interact, each intensifying the other," said W. D. Wall. He also suggests that some causes of failure spring directly from teachers' techniques.

Although the authors have suggested that freely chosen and richly equipped play often helps to resolve emotional difficulties, and free mental energy for learning, this is not the whole picture. It is far more complex than that.

Referring to backwardness in reading, Wall remarks, "An examination of the evidence suggests that emotional disturbance is sometimes the cause, sometimes the result and sometimes the concomitant of reading difficulty."[1] In other words, tension may enter the picture in any or all of three ways. Family Grouping helps the slow child by minimizing the difference between his attainment and that of others in his class. He is more likely to feel at ease because, proceeding at his own pace, he is less conspicuous than he would be in a class of children of his own age. Since a feeling of failure undoubtedly begets failure, this is in itself valuable. Here, prevention and cure go hand in hand.

But Wall further remarks that "there are more problems of maladjustment among intelligent children who are failing in school than amongst less intelligent groups". Here he is speaking of older children. But all these children have been Infants. Were they, perhaps, as intellectually able children, hurried on too fast and not given enough opportunity to play or to resolve in self-initiated ways problems which later re-presented themselves? Or have they never become fully involved in the wish to learn, but followed intellectual pursuits to please parent or teacher?

This brings us to the last aspect of emotional development with which this chapter will deal.

Motivation for Learning

We find a precise statement by Wall: "Children will learn because they are emotionally stirred by the situation in which they find themselves."[2]

The emotions stirred may be of various kinds; a child working for fear of punishment is stirred by emotion; so also is one doing so purely to please his teacher; or later, in order to beat his class-mates in the class list.

Is there any one emotion which we would wish the young child to

---

[1] W. Wall, F. Schonell, W. Olsen: *Failure in School.*
[2] W. Wall: *Education and Mental Health.*

associate with learning? Surely, for the sake of his immediate and future ego-involvement in learning it must be that of *pleasure*.

In the pleasure which children have in finding out new things, and extending their knowledge and skills, a teacher has her greatest ally. Every child is strongly motivated to master adult skills, and do what older, more clever and more powerful people do.

As the teacher provides step after step in a new world of developing skills, linking them to the self-directed drive of chosen experience, a sound work attitude on which later achievement will rest is slowly being developed. Once again the responsible task of the Infants' teacher reaches far beyond the child's classroom.

"The development of a sound work attitude which is compounded of confidence in one's own power to succeed and the willingness to accept immediate drudgery for a worthwhile end, is one of the major mental health and educational goals of the primary school."[1]

What are the implications of this for us in school? We suggest they are:

1. Confidence in one's own power to succeed *only* follows success.

Children should not be put into a position of failure: sums should *always* be right or they are too difficult for the sumster: reading success must be at the level, however simple, which a child can manage. He will gladly move on if he is being successful. A long-term goal is invisible to the Infants' school child.

2. "Acceptance of drudgery for the sake of a worthwhile end." What meaning can this have for an Infant?

It may be slogging at a dull, time-consuming part of a model, or rewriting a story for a group magazine, or sorting pictures for a book or practising a skill. These tasks he will accept as worthwhile. But there is plenty of drudgery and little end that a child sees as worthwhile in some of the repetitive tasks he is asked to undertake. Arranging cardboard letters to form teacher-dictated words, or copying out sentences of news which someone else has originated produce the attitude that school work has to be undertaken to please the teacher or to keep busy for the sake of keeping quiet instead of the other way round.

3. The principle of proceeding slowly and establishing each plateau of learning is an absolutely basic one for the young learner. Attitudes of "confidence in tackling new learning, the willingness to take a risk . . . the power to digest failure when it comes, or to try again, depend upon an experience in which success has predominated."[2]

---

[1] W. Wall: *Education and Mental Health.*
[2] W. Wall, F. Schonell, W. Olson: *Failure in School.*

These words should be stamped on a plaque on the desk of every Infants' teacher. It is partly upon the attitudes towards learning developed in the Infants' school that the future mental health of the adult depends.

Consider the following table of emotions accompanying success or failure in intellectual activity:

SUCCESS	FAILURE
satisfaction	disappointment
self-confidence	fear
pride in achievement	limitation
love of object overcome	hatred of object or rival
positive self-feeling	negative self-feeling

It hardly requires enlarging upon. It is inevitable that a child meets with both success and failure, but "continual thwarting" or fear in some form "produces a shrinking attitude towards experience".

How vitally important it is then for the Infants' teacher to prevent the experience of failure, and to recognize the supreme importance of ego-involvement, and active self-motivation in play and work (see Chapter 5).

In 1927 the following words were written by Dr. M. J. Reavey: "When we consider how for years small children have been kept sitting passively in desks for several hours a day . . . we may realize the harm that has unwittingly been done. The apathy, lack of interest and power of concentration that we see so prevalent is probably the direct result of such a mistake."[1] Is it not true to say such mistakes are still all too frequently being made?

When we listen to the voice of the expert, "Satisfactory human development depends upon the success with which the fundamental emotional needs of each individual are met within the framework of the society in which he grows up,"[2] we realize afresh that teachers wield enormous power. They virtually control the society in which small children spend so great a proportion of their time. In order to meet its needs for "satisfactory human development" they need flexibility of mind, the insight to see what those needs are and the ability to provide the means by which children can help themselves and be helped.

This requires considerable sensitivity. The teacher's part is to be neither an onlooker nor a participant; willing to contribute if need be, yet not too anxious to organize. Above all a teacher needs faith

---

[1] M. Reavey: *The Place of Play in Education.*
[2] W. Wall: *Education and Mental Health.*

in what she is doing, and a complete conviction that it is worthwhile.

No system has yet been devised which is completely adequate for the child's or the teacher's needs; however, Family Grouping is more adequate than most.

4

Social Development

The social climate (of a school) is of fundamental importance, for on it depend the attitudes which determine whether children are to grow into creative democrats, autocratic authoritarians, apathetic conformists or dangerous rebels.[1]

Social Growth

"Intellectual development may lead to some satisfaction but it can never lead to a full and happy life unless it is accompanied by sound emotional and social development. Good social development is dependent on the satisfactory relationship of a child with his mother and with other adults and children whom he meets in early childhood. The degree to which a child has dealt satisfactorily with his nuclear feelings of love, hate and jealousy in early childhood will determine the nature of his social relationships at adolescence."[2]

Children of pre-school age tend to be solitary. In a nursery school children play together in twos and threes in a parallel fashion, but they are self-centred and unable to play really cooperatively. Real attachments are more likely to be with an adult rather than with their school-mates.

The writer had occasion to enter a nursery class where groups of children were engaged in various table activities with their teacher. The teacher left the table, and within two or three minutes the groups had disintegrated, having lost the support of the adult. This is typical of the pre-school child.

When a child enters the Infants' school he is still mainly interested in himself and his own part in any activity. He is, however, ready for some cooperative play. At about the age of 5 plus, friendships begin to develop. Whereas it is normal for the pre-school child and the new entrant to play alone, the solitary child of 6 should give rise to some concern. As the child gets older, his dependence on the adult decreases and he relies more and more on his fellows for companionship. At first friendships fluctuate a good deal, but by the age of 7 many children begin to form some firm friendships which can last for a number of years.

Good social development cannot be 'taught' in the classroom. It is

---

[1] A. Hughes: *Education and the Democratic Ideal.*
[2] A. Bowley: *The Natural Development of the Child.*

dependent on maturation and experience. Susan Isaacs, describing the way in which children of the Maltinghouse School were influenced towards such desirable behaviour as gentle manners, positive consideration for others, and active social cooperation, says, "These things refuse dictation, but they grow in response to the friendliness and reliability of the adult, and happy reciprocal relations with other children. To have permanent value they must be spontaneous and spring from a happy free friendliness."[1] To provide an environment which will encourage the growth of good social relationships is one of the prime responsibilities of teachers.

Social Experience

Family-grouped classes provide a much wider variety of social experiences than the Traditionally-grouped class, particularly where they are based on the Free Day which encourages the maximum intermingling of various age-groups. The 5-year-old child will have many opportunities to experiment with his approaches to other children. He will also have opportunity to experience willing help given by older children and their readiness to make allowances for the 'little one's' immaturities. Older children look forward to the arrival of the new ones and show much tenderness towards them. Because they are nearer their age, they seem better able than an adult to comfort the new arrivals if they are miserable during their first few days away from home.

In a Family-grouped class it is also noticeable that 5-year-olds do not cling to the teacher as they do in a Reception class where the teacher is the only person of greater maturity. It needs little or no suggestion from the teacher to encourage older children to offer help when it is needed. Older children are only too ready to demonstrate their greater skill at tying shoe laces, doing up buttons, attending to minor accidents, clearing up and the many other jobs that crop up in the classroom. Not only does this relieve the teacher of such tasks, but it provides valuable social training for the children. Younger children are left more free to develop at their own rate. The teacher does not need to make as many demands on them as she would if there were no older children in the class capable of taking responsibility. Because children have a strong natural urge to become independent, there is little danger that they will become over-dependent.

As the children become more mature and experienced they naturally take more responsibility for themselves and the class. Many young children have been seen to refuse help once they are able to manage themselves. The next step is to help those who are less able than themselves. Development is a very slow process and may hardly be noticed by the teacher, but it is very apparent when new children join the class.

[1] S. Isaacs: *Intellectual Growth in Young Children.*

E

In a Traditionally-grouped class it is easy for slow or backward children to feel inferior unless they possess some non-academic ability which gives them an opportunity to excel. They may be rejected by their more able fellows and become socially or emotionally upset. Some may even resort to unacceptable behaviour in their endeavour to make an impression. This seldom happens in a Family-grouped class, however. By the time a child is old enough to realize that he is not progressing academically as rapidly as other children, there will be other younger children in the class who are able to do even less. This can help to lessen the child's sense of inferiority. It is even more beneficial if he can be encouraged to help the younger members of the class.

One 7-year-old boy, very immature and backward in his reading, experienced great pleasure in helping the 'little ones' with their reading. He regarded it as his special job. Not only did this reinforce his own knowledge, but it gave him a sense of responsibility and satisfaction which he would not otherwise have had.

Older children who may have made little progress with intellectual subjects derive great satisfaction from using their greater social maturity to organize groups of younger children in non-intellectual activities. This is particularly noticeable in play with such materials as bricks, constructional toys, sand and water. Children with little intellectual ability use their greater general maturity and show considerable imagination in this type of play. Thus the play of the younger children is enriched, whilst the older child has an opportunity to experience success and satisfaction at being able to play a leading role.

Teachers of mixed-age classes frequently make such comments as, "We hardly ever seem to have behaviour problems," and this may be because the situation gives plenty of opportunity for legitimate ego-building achievement.

Outlet and Opportunity

Although Family Grouping does provide an environment which will aid children whose development diverges from what may be regarded as normal, it is important to be sure that the best possible environment is provided for *all* children. There will be almost as wide a range of personalities as there are children in the class, but Charlotte Bühler[1] distinguishes personality types from children's social behaviour as follows:

1. Leaders—those children displaying sufficient initiative and talent to make suggestions and attract followers.

2. Helpers—children who look for other children whom they can help and lend things to.

---

[1] C. Bühler: *From Birth to Maturity*.

3. Maternal children—who seek out and take care of their weaker and more helpless neighbours.

4. The favourites—characteristic of the youngest members of the school group. Usually kind, gentle and charming children who make little effort to establish contact with the others, but who, nevertheless, are the recipients of all kinds of attention from them.

5. Despotic children—who tyrannize others.

6. Children who joke and make fun of others; children who are constantly showing off.

7. Social failures—children who are physically defective, dirty or poorly dressed and may be ostracized by others.

All these categories are provided for admirably in a Family-grouped class.

There is plenty of scope for the leader to make use of his initiative and capacity to organize groups of children in their various activities. Young children often like to have an older child to organize their games, and their play is enriched by the greater maturity of the older leader. In a class where all the children are about 7 years, the number of natural leaders is likely to be too large for the number of opportunities for leadership which arise within the class. As a result competition and antagonism seem to spring up more frequently than in a Family-grouped class where there will be fewer children possessing the quality of leadership and a very much greater opportunity for them to make use of this quality. As one teacher wrote, "Jealousies and hurt feelings seem to occur more frequently when there are lots of children of one age."

Most 7-year-olds come into Charlotte Bühler's second category at some time or another, and many of them frequently ask for jobs to do. In a class where all the children are the same age it is impossible for all of them to have the satisfaction of being useful. Where only a third of the children are in this age-group there are fewer children to share jobs and more children needing help. It is possible for all the older children to have the experience of feeling responsible.

A Family-grouped class provides the ideal environment for maternal children. There are always younger children who benefit from mothering, as well as the weaker more helpless ones among the older children.

The despotic child who tyrannizes over others can sometimes be a difficult problem. Family Grouping cannot always solve this problem, but it is true to say that the presence of younger children does bring out a tenderness in most of the older children. Children who tyrannize others do so sometimes through feelings of insecurity. They see other children as a threat to themselves and are constantly on the defensive. Younger children do not constitute quite such a threat, and therefore provide opportunity for more friendly relationships to build up.

Children who fall into the seventh category—the social failures—are perhaps the ones who gain most from Family Grouping. Few children of Infants' school age are ostracized by others. Nowadays few children come to school dirty or poorly dressed and except in extreme cases, those who look uncared for are accepted by the others. Young children are usually sympathetic towards any member of the class who has a physical defect. In a Family-grouped class where there is maximum encouragement for children to help each other this is even more marked (see Chapter 3).

One of the most important benefits of Family Grouping is in the sphere of personal attainment. Children are sympathetic to each other and competition is virtually eliminated. Children realize that work produced is valued for its own sake and is not to be compared with work done by other children. The younger ones often admire the work of the older ones, but equally the 7-year-olds will praise the work of the younger children. Comments such as, "He read that book right through by himself," or "He's clever for 5, isn't he?" are frequent.

Children do sometimes envy the clever ones and try to keep up with them, but there is no sense of rivalry or sense of failure if they do not succeed, since the emphasis is always on improving their own individual standard. This lack of competition also saves the clever child from being ostracized by the others because he is 'too clever' and helps him remain a member of the group because he learns that some less clever children have capabilities which he himself lacks.

One amusing story illustrates this point. During the dinner break two 7-year-old girls had stayed to wash the painting easels. They were both very nice girls, but one was clever and the other was not making much progress with academic work but was quite self-confident and constantly chattering. The writer recorded the following conversation.

1st Child: "Do you like doing jobs?"

2nd Child: "Yes."

1st Child: "So do I. I'm good at doing jobs. See, you're good at reading and writing and doing sums, but you're not so good at doing this. I'm not very good at reading and those things, but I'm good at jobs like this . . . It's good to do jobs like this. When you're grown up, see, someone has to do jobs like washing the stinking socks, don't they?"

Sibling Relationships

Should members of the same family be placed in the same class? Teachers' opinions differ on this. In some schools siblings are deliberately kept apart because teachers feel that timid children may gain confidence away from more dominant siblings. Others feel that there are older members of some families who are required to carry heavy responsibility for their younger brothers and sisters already, and that to be in the same class with them adds unnecessarily to this strain.

68

Still others fear that the natural sibling rivalries of home life may be carried into school. A brief consideration of the causes of such rivalry, however, shows that this is less likely to occur than would first appear.

The different demands made by siblings of various ages on members of the family, and in particular on the mother, often cause jealousy and rivalry among brothers and sisters, however careful parents may be in trying to avoid it. It is hard for the older child to see his place being taken by a new baby; he is not sufficiently mature to realize that his gain in greater independence and responsibility is vitally necessary if he is to grow into a well-adjusted adult.

A young child wants it both ways; he wants to grow up and be independent yet he still needs his mother's love, and he fails to understand that his mother will go on loving him as well as caring for the new baby. Naturally he resents the new intruder and has to learn gradually to accept him. In this he is helped by increased responsibility, particularly if his mother is wise in allowing this to take the form of sharing in the care of the baby. Later, it will be the baby's turn to show jealousy. Whilst he is proud of his older brother, and enjoys his company, there are bound to be times when jealousy arises as a result of the extra privileges allowed to an older child.

Where there are three or more children in the family it can be even more difficult for those who come in the middle. When a third child arrives the second sibling suddenly becomes aware that his very close mother-baby relationship has come to an end, but he does not have the compensation of being the oldest child with the greater privileges. In addition, it is more than likely that the oldest child (as well as his mother) will, for a time at least, turn his attention more towards the newest arrival. It is little wonder that relationships between siblings are far from harmonious at times, and that social adjustment to each other takes time.

The focal point of these sibling tensions is the child-mother-child relationship. Removed to the less emotionally charged environment of school, the rivals are often able to make good progress towards an amicable relationship, and rivalry feelings are supplanted by those of admiration, protection and mutual pride.

Siblings normally overcome their jealousy and often in the process develop a warm affection for each other. Parents, watching some piece of amiable sibling cooperation, will often say, astonished, "Good gracious! They fight like cat and dog at home!"

Some adults have said, "I hated the sight of my brother or sister when I was at school, and would have hated to have had him or her in the same class." But actually this seems to be unusual rather than a common situation. It has been observed over and over again in a Traditionally-grouped school that where a younger brother or sister comes to school the older child shows anxiety about him, and if not allowed legitimately to see him, will seek an excuse to get into his classroom. At playtime and home times he anxiously waits to help him with his clothes and to make sure all is well.

Many a young child coming to school for the first time has looked bewildered at the sight of so many unknown faces. He may have been looking forward to joining his older brother at school and will have been disappointed to find that in fact he was not with him. Some teachers would say, "He has to get used to being on his own." This may be true but it is the teacher's task to see that it is done naturally, by easy stages, without a great emotional upset.

In a very large family sibling jealousies are probably more diffuse since it is less likely that such intense relationships develop between children, and the mother's love and affection is observed to be spread more widely over the whole family. In addition, brothers and sisters have had more opportunity to learn to give and take, and share their possessions.

The Family-grouped class has some of the advantages of the large family. Children with younger brothers and sisters at home look forward to their coming to school and constantly talk about it. When the time arrives they proudly take responsibility, show them round the classroom and initiate them into the new world. The little one feels secure straight away. Feelings of jealousy seldom show in these first few vital days. Instead one sees the growth of mutual affection as the older child initiates the younger one into school life, to some extent taking the mother's place by helping with the things which still are difficult, such as doing up buttons. Some young children like to bring a favourite toy to school for the first few weeks. In forming a link between home and school this is a great comfort. But how much more comforting to be with one's own brother or sister.

Within a few weeks, provided the children are well-adjusted, they will make friends among other members of the class. They may not associate much with siblings but, except in a small minority of cases, it has been found that they like to be in the same classroom and seldom quarrel.

It is possible that for some children jealous feelings are lessened when the second child reaches school age. When the oldest child goes to school he may feel rejected and resent the fact that his younger brother or sister is still at home receiving all his mother's attention. In some cases where children do not settle in school, investigations show that the problem lies in the child's reluctance to leave his mother and a younger sibling rather than in any real dislike for school.

One instance of this can be quoted.

"Jane was the eldest of three children, the youngest of whom died. There was only about eleven months' difference in age between Jane and her younger brother John and she was very jealous, although outwardly fond of him. She did not settle down well when she first went to school; she became enuretic and would not eat dinner at school. Her position in the family had probably meant that she had to be independent at a very early age and she had resented no longer being the baby, going to school, and leaving John at home with mother. She was relieved when he came to school. John was in the same class and Jane knew where he was and could see he was not having more maternal attention than she. He was a clever little boy and she was able to get satisfaction from the opportunity to show pride in his achievements. The two children played together quite frequently and Jane made a lot of fuss of her brother and enjoyed looking after him. John liked to know Jane was around even when not playing with her. Both children were helped by the other's presence. Their relationships at home improved considerably."

One headteacher, whilst placing brothers and sisters together, prefers to separate twins. Such cases as this must always be considered individually. Where twins are of the same sex and very much alike there is a tendency on the part of their mothers to make them appear as much alike as possible, although they may have completely different personalities. In such cases it may be hard for the children to establish their own identity and it could benefit them to be in separate classes.

Another headteacher feels that where one twin is more intelligent than the other it is better to separate them to avoid emphasizing feelings of inferiority or superiority. In such cases it would seem kinder to allow the children to remain together, for at least a short period, to enable them to get used to the atmosphere of school.

Some twins are so entirely different from each other that they will establish their own identity almost from birth, and may have much to offer each other. This was true of one pair of twins—a boy and a girl. They were both very timid on coming to school, particularly the boy, who was much bigger than his sister. For the first few weeks they clung to each other and would not be parted, but the little girl then lost her shyness and started to mix with the other children. The boy always stayed near her and was upset if she went out of the room for a few minutes.

However, gradually he became more confident and made friends among the other boys. Being the more intelligent of the two children he began to gain satisfaction from progress in the basic skills, and developed into a quiet studious child. His sister was entirely different, gaining her satisfaction from her social activities in the classroom. Both children remained devoted to each other and showed pride in each other's achievements, but both had developed along completely independent lines.

On the whole, the Family-grouped class provides the opportunity for brothers and sisters to learn toleration towards each other away from the tension which arises in the home. In the broader environment of the classroom contact between siblings is less intense than in the home, and they do not see each other as a threat to their own position.

One of the main advantages of Family Grouping is its flexibility. There need be no hard and fast rule on the placing of members of the same family together, since it is an easy matter to transfer children from one class to another should this be felt necessary.

A situation which sometimes calls for transfer is that where the younger member of the family is of markedly superior intelligence to the older one. Tensions and inferior feelings may build up in the older child when the younger, more intelligent brother or sister begins to surpass him in attainment, especially if unfavourable attention is drawn to the fact by adults at home or at school. If the older child is moved on to another classroom this tension is eased, the opportunity for direct comparison lessened and the older sibling's confidence can be restored in more subtle ways.

A long period of contact with the same family gives a teacher considerable insight into parental attitudes and domestic situations. She comes to know the whole family, and through such knowledge achieves a better understanding of the needs of the children she teaches. Parents have growing confidence in her as they come to know her better, and feel free to discuss their aspirations or difficulties concerning their children.

Relationships Between Children of Different Ages

"The spontaneous groupings which take place on the playground are primarily determined by maturity factors."[1]

It is probably true that generally children seek their closest friends among children of the same age. This is only to be expected, because as children develop, their interests change and it is natural that they should look for companions of similar maturity and similar interests.

But it may be that we ourselves have been partly responsible for encouraging the segregation of the various age-groups. The headmaster of a rural school said, "In larger schools the age-groups seem to play separately, even in the playground, whereas in village schools child lore, songs, games and so on have survived, having been passed on from older to younger children as they played naturally together."

Children, naturally, make most of their friends among the children they meet in their own class. If the classes are grouped according to age it is not surprising that friendships tend to be between children of the same age. Where children are organized in Family groups there is a great deal of intermixing both in the classroom and in the playground, particularly if they are given a Free Day.

---

[1] A. Gesell and F. Ilg: *The Child from Five to Ten.*

Cooperation v. Competition

One very large group of boys chose to play with the big bricks every morning over a period of several weeks. Several boys had brought toy soldiers and cowboys to school and set up rival camps. Naturally the game consisted of attacks and counter-attacks between different camps, but although the essence of the game was rivalry, it never degenerated into genuine quarrelling between the children. The amount of co-operation was surprising and such polite remarks as, "Please may I have that big brick?" were frequently heard. Although the composition of the group fluctuated slightly from day to day, it generally consisted of about a dozen children, with about one third of them falling into each age-group.

Observation of a mixed age-group engaged on various activities shows that there is a considerable amount of this type of cooperation going on all the time. The 'home corner' lends itself to this type of cooperation, but mixed groups will also be seen in the reading corner, the number corner and in fact anywhere where cooperation is needed.

Model making and project work particularly call for cooperation. The younger children are willing helpers. They are often pleased to do jobs which some of the older children would find monotonous, such as tearing paper, pasting, or painting backgrounds for group pictures. One group of 5-year-olds thoroughly enjoyed making very simple little people to form the audience of a model circus made mainly by the 6 and 7-year-olds.

When making models, a younger child will often work with an older one, and in so doing learn techniques which he in turn will pass on. With a large project several children may work together, as in the making of a model ship. "Two 7-year-olds worked together on this for several days. They were then joined by two other children who painted the sea on which to stand the ship. Later some matchsticks were required to make rails. These were brought by a 5-year-old who had apparently shown no previous interest in the ship. This boy, with one of the 7-year-olds and another 5-year-old, carefully stuck the matches round the edge of the ship, but they were insufficient to go right round. The 7-year-old boy took out the ones which were too close together and spread them more evenly so that there were sufficient to go right round. This process took some time, but it was closely watched by a third 5-year-old boy who joined the group without taking any active part."

Many similar examples could be quoted, but just one more will be given here: "Several of the older girls were busy making little story books, stitching the pages together with cotton. Some of the little children became interested and started making picture books on similar lines. The teacher promised to help them with the sewing, but could not get round to the group for some time. Meanwhile, the older girls went to the rescue and stitched up the books for the younger children."

The following quotation brings out the importance of fostering cooperation as against competition in the classroom. "Where children are constantly being helped to appreciate one another's gifts rather than compete with each other for supremacy there will be little or none of the bullying amongst boys or spitefulness amongst girls that frequently occurs in schools which emphasize rivalry . . . It is heartening to find that the teacher's respect for the children as persons is reflected in the sensitivity and helpfulness shown by these children to one another. Schools can, in fact, teach children how to live constructively with one another much more effectively now than formerly, when they attempted to teach the glory of surpassing one's neighbour and the duty of loving him as oneself at the same time."[1]

---

[1] H. James and others: *Periods of Stress in the Primary School.*

5

Intellectual Development

Maturation × Experience = Achievement.[1]

Indications of Intellectual Growth

"How does Family Grouping affect intellectual attainment?" is a recurring question asked of teachers who work in this way. The questioners really mean, "Do the three Rs suffer?"

This is a valid question. Every teacher is concerned that her pupils should show the best results. The answer to the question must obviously be "No"—or at any rate, "Not ultimately", or teachers would not wish to work in this way. Teachers who use Vertical Age-grouping do so, as must be becoming clear, because of a conviction that children's capacities are ultimately better developed as a result.

When modern informal methods are in use, whether in Family-grouped classes or not, new criteria are called for in measuring the results which they give. We no longer judge by the capacity to produce neat copy to someone else's writing, or a page of correct, mechanically worked sums, or even to read the last book in a reading scheme. Of course one of the aims of Infant Education is that children should be able to read, and read well, but far more than that is wanted.

Intellectual growth means development in the skill of thinking; true thinking in its various modes includes reasoning, judgment, creativity, reflection and intuition as well as memorization. Infant children are capable of all these—at their own level. Generally speaking, this level is one of practical performance. If infants have the opportunity to perform all these mental operations at the level which is correct for their stage of development, their individual mental growth is facilitated, and their ultimate level of performance is more likely to be the highest of which they are capable, than if they are restricted to formal or abstract learning through repetitive, teacher-directed tasks.

Very high standards of reading, number, free writing and investigation into the world of things (the beginning of science) develop in Family-grouped classrooms, along with other desirable personality attributes.

---

[1] W. Wall, F. Schonell, W. Olson: *Failure in School.*

A Sample Situation

Let us take a look at a sample situation such as might be found by a visitor to a Family-grouped classroom. 5, 6 and 7-year-old children might be seen engaged in the following activities:

A group working at a model, perhaps of a dockside scene, with ships, cranes, warehouses and a system of railway tracks.

Two children looking up information related to the model, perhaps using an atlas or the globe.

Another looking up different kinds of ships in a reference book such as the *Observer's Book of Ships*.

Another copying the inner view of a cargo boat.

A group, dressed up, playing in the home corner.

A 7-year-old girl reading to two younger ones.

Two older children playing Scrabble.

Two others playing Snakes and Ladders, or some similar number game.

Younger children sorting and threading beads, using pegboard or doing jigsaw puzzles.

Others painting.

A group cutting out pictures from magazines ready to illustrate a scrapbook on fluids—following an interest which started with water play.

A group at the sand tray.

Some constructing with big blocks and bricks.

A few doing handwriting practice (perhaps tracing, copying or decorating).

Two or three writing and illustrating their own stories.

Two or three measuring themselves with tape-measures and recording the results.

One or two carrying out the routine tasks of attending to plants, recording the day's temperature or feeding the class pet.

It may be difficult to see the teacher at first; she may be sitting at a table discussing peg-board patterns with two or three 5-year-olds, or outside the room altogether fetching fresh material. If she should rise to talk, the children continue unconcerned with their tasks.

The visitor may ask, "How is all this kept going?" and again, "How can you be sure that every child is usefully occupied and making progress in the three Rs?" The answer to the first question is, "Organization" and the second, "Records".

Below the Surface

What are these children doing, other than the obvious tasks upon which they are engaged? They are:

Taking pleasure in school and its possibilities for work and play.

Acquiring the ability to concentrate for long spells.

Selecting self-initiated programmes and following them through to the utmost extent of their talents (using reading, writing and calculating if they have these skills and they are appropriate).

Taking steps towards creative thinking and problem-solving.

Exercising judgment.

Seeking and classifying information and finding out 'how to find out' using an atlas, picture dictionary or reference book.

Performing purposeful routine tasks such as cleaning or tidying, feeding the hamster or recording what food he has had.

Learning to order knowledge to extract further information. "Look on the chart and find the tallest child." Read the book about Chippy the Hamster and find out what food he had yesterday.

Adding to their individual structure of abilities, e.g. forming a growing vocabulary, either spoken or written.

Building positive social relationships and strengthening their own emotional harmony (see Chapters 3 and 4).

Taking a measure of responsibility for their own learning. Older children know that some practice at the skills is required of them each day. We cannot yet tell what implications this may have for future educational developments such as the use of teaching machines.

Giving the watchful teacher a number of clues as to starting points for future development such as a play to act, with written invitations to other classes, or an accompanied visit to the local library or some other place of interest.

What to do

Although some teachers may feel that such a classroom in full and active operation may be very worthwhile, they wonder how it is to be achieved, or feel intimidated at such a prospect.

Discussing organization with teachers and watching them at work makes it clear that at least four basic principles are usual.

1. *Provide a wealth of opportunities*

These are based on the intellectual skills of reading, writing and number; on creative work of every kind, and on play (see Chapter 3). Children must know what the possibilities are. Even where they help themselves to the equipment or material it is inevitable that some equipment is more to the fore and used most frequently. Children who enjoy certain types of activity, such as painting, jig-saw puzzles or reading, may because of concentration upon them miss other pleasant, important or stimulating pastimes altogether; interesting equipment may be overlooked. The perceptive teacher guides and suggests and she herself may sit down to work with a neglected number game, or to read a book. She will be quickly joined.

2. *Have a routine and see that the children know it*

Some teachers start the day with a required task until registration and other routine jobs are over. Others allow children to make a free choice as soon as they arrive. Others have specific periods when older children must pay special attention to the academic skills, or perhaps a half-hour when particular help is given to the 5-year-olds. In all cases, the children know the routine as thoroughly as the teacher, and round this stable framework the day's doings revolve. Some teachers explain that they began with a fairly tight routine which they have been able to modify as they and the children became acclimatized to an informal way of working.

3. *Have confidence in the children*

Given the opportunities, children will take them. No longer has the impetus for work to be provided mainly by the teacher. "The 'activity' movement is no mere passing fashion; it is a sincere attempt to use the creative energy of children."[1] Children, unlike inhibited adults, do not have to "think what to make" or "think what to do", except when they have only just been introduced to this way of working, or where the materials are poor and inadequate. The best results come from the most varied materials; children only ask, "What shall I do?" when the possibilities for interesting activity are insufficient.

Miss Brearley asks us to "watch what happens, for example, when you add some little bits of fur and sequins to the needlework table. You can see the children's minds opening to take in new opportunities and their immediate response in the increased imagination and complexity of their work".[2] Provision of fresh material is one of the most important ways by which the teacher stimulates intellectual development.

4. *Watch for fresh opportunities to arise—and use them*

It has been said, "The act of making something stimulates a lively flows of ideas and images."[3] Children do not lack ideas. If the teacher's own mind is alert to the possibilities which children themselves present, she can indicate ways in which these ideas may grow and expand.

Attention is paid later in this chapter to such 'starting points'. Having noted them, the teacher talks with the children about them, and helps them to go farther.

---

[1] A. Hughes: *Education and the Democratic Ideal.*
[2] M. Brearley: *Studies in Education: First Years in School: The Practical Implications for the Teacher.*
[3] C. Bühler: *From Birth to Maturity.*

Simpson comments: "We have found, through these discussions, where the children's real interests lie, and we have been fascinated to lead them, through their own questions and their own thirst for information, into the realms of History, Geography, Biology, Local History and General Knowledge."[1] Other children notice, and those who are ready will join in.

The 'follow-through' of an interest is not difficult provided that a teacher's mind is flexible. The difficulty is sometimes to know which of the many possibilities to pursue. Some teachers inexperienced in such methods wonder how to get started. They should bear in mind that "activities are much more effective than conversation in provoking problems",[2] and when giving the children the chance to experiment, should play and work with them.

Getting On

Before dealing with the skills of reading, writing and number, it may be as well to consider the question: "Is there any positive way to be sure that progress is being made—that a child is not wasting his time?" Although records (see Chapter 7) are the most positive indication of progress in learning, there are also some general clues which may help to guide the teacher. Ask the following questions:

1. Is the child physically healthy, lively and alert?

2. Does he show enthusiasm? Is he enjoying school in general, or any activity in particular?

3. Does he show progress in his choices (over a period of time relative to the two to three years he will spend in the class), or does he always build the same model, paint the same picture, or wear the same dressing-up clothes? If he does (subject to the remarks on page 51), it looks as though the teacher must provide the stimulus to a more advanced stage of work or play, or open the door to some new interest.

4. Is he talking more fluently, with a developing vocabulary?

5. Is he growing more confident, friendly, helpful and stable in his relationships with other children and with adults?

6. Does he exhibit willingness to tackle something new, and is he prepared to persevere until he has finished it?

Particularly pertinent to the question of perseverance is the willingness of a teacher to let children carry on with something which is giving them satisfaction. For instance, children who are just finding fluency in reading like to spend a very long time in the book corner. A particularly absorbing model or piece of dramatic play should be allowed

---

[1] D. Simpson and D. Alderson: *Creative Play in the Infants' School.*
[2] S. Isaacs: *Intellectual Growth in Young Children.*

to run its natural course, however time-consuming. Children will often be willing afterwards to work hard at a routine task in order to master a skill or technique.

Some children will go ahead fast in all the ways listed, but most will go forward unevenly, with the emphasis first here, then there, and with occasional regressions in some area. A very few will appear to be stuck and may need the expert help of a doctor or psychologist.

The Skills of Language—Talking

Talking, drawing, writing and reading are inseparable. They are all forms of communication and the first two are fundamental human activities. Most 5-year-olds come to school able to talk, and with a passionate interest in drawing and scribbling. These are the starting points to language development.

It has been suggested that a child needs a vocabulary of 3,000 words before he should begin to learn to read. Watts tells us that, "we may assume a vocabulary of 2,000 words at five, developing to 4,000 at seven plus."[1] A child does not acquire such a vocabulary merely by listening. Language develops best through talk with adults and with other children. The teacher makes conscious contributions to the growing vocabulary with stories and poetry, by arranging meaningful experiences, and through conversation with individuals and groups. This is a major part of an Infant teacher's work, and one which has been misunderstood and neglected in the past.

The old style 'conversation lesson' was unnatural and inhibiting to all but the most extrovert children. In the Infant classroom conversation should be continuous. When children have used words in talk, and actively made them their own, the words become part of their mental equipment, available for manipulation in thought.

Three boys, two 6-year-olds and one 5, were building a ship with large blocks. They were inside the structure, explaining excitedly to their teacher, "I'm the captain and he's the second captain and he's the third captain. And you turn the steering wheel and the ship goes and the waves get big and come in the windows, and the thing-on-the-bottom gets broken and the ship stops . . ." Within the space of a few minutes, by interested but apparently casual conversation, the teacher added five new words to their vocabulary—lieutenant, bridge, helm, porthole and propeller. In the excitement of the self-created situation, the boys lapped up the new language. It was one of the chances for which the teacher was looking as part of her teaching technique.

We have in the past expected children to put much into writing which they could scarcely express in speech and this discouraged creati-

---

[1] A. Watts: *The Language and Mental Development of the Child.*

Mixed-age group of girls playing "foot-strings" (see pages 52 and 72), and a mixed-age group of boys at brick play

Cooperation: joint creative work consolidates good relationships between brothers of 5 and 7 years

vity and stifled originality. Before children acquire fluency in talking, reading and writing, no less than three sets of symbols have to be mastered.[1] It is an enormous intellectual task, but we take it so much for granted. Sometimes small reference is made to the fact when backwardness is being discussed, even though educationalists have been aware of it for many years. Said Pestalozzi, "He must be able to speak about many things before he can read books intelligently."

Children with gross speech difficulties usually receive expert help, but many children leave the Infants' school inarticulate. A naturally reserved child will be no worse off for being reserved, but there are probably many children whose poverty of self-expression in later years originates in the "don't talk" régimes of early school life. The two most natural things for young children to do are to move about and to talk. How often their spontaneity is inhibited by the "Now we'll all sit down and be quiet" approach. But children whose natural physical liveliness and verbal intercourse is normally unfettered will accept sensibly and willingly an occasional embargo on free talk or movement if there is a special reason for it.

The Skills of Language—Drawing

Scribbling and drawing is another natural medium of communication for young children, the origins of which lie deep in our subconscious. By it ideas are discussed, experience clarified and emotional adjustments made. Plenty of opportunity should be given for drawing, scribbling and painting, but the drawing and scribbling should not be looked upon as a 'time-waster' either by a child or his teacher. From the start of school life the 5-year-old should be given a folder of stout paper in which to keep his drawing. Some schools provide a large scribble pad: loose sheets can be stapled together, and a cover made on which the child writes his name—"John Adams: First Book".

In due time a second book can be started. Now comes an important step towards a child evaluating his own work. The books form a basis of discussion with the teacher, or perhaps with the group. A favourite page may be chosen (a value judgment is being made) and "My Best Page" written on it: an older child will help number the pages in order. Soon, quite a young child will be doing this for himself (acquisition of number symbols). Then comes the chance to add writing to a page of special importance—"This is my new car"—and a new step forward is made.

The steps in progression are:

(a) Staple separate sheets to make books.

(b) Name and number the pages and books with help from the teacher or an older child.

---

[1] For a discussion of the acquisition of spoken and written symbols the reader is referred to S. Orton: *Reading, Writing and Speech Problems in Children.*

(c) Make value judgments concerning best or favourite pages. A child can see for himself his own advance. The teacher can suggest various media for use: crayons, pencil, charcoal, tracing or cutting and sticking and different types of paper. Different shapes should also be available.

(d) The teacher adds some writing which is traced over or copied by the child. Some teachers later give a child a 'teachers' work book' in which she writes and from which he copies.

Care should be taken that only a limited amount of writing is based on drawing or painting. The practice of requiring a child to write something about every picture he draws carries this otherwise useful teaching device to absurd lengths. As L. Hollamby remarks, "Creativity is inhibited, as children have one eye on the caption."[1] A child might well be tempted to think, "Surely what I have to say is plain enough in the picture." By the same token the question, "What is it?" should never be asked of a child's painting, drawing or model. If the message is not obvious then the invitation, "Tell me about it," will show interest and stimulate talk without the subtle overtone of suggested criticism.

It is worthwhile taking trouble making these early books. They give great satisfaction and confidence to the young entrant, who feels his work important from the start.

Many teachers have commented on the value to a child of entering a Family-grouped class, where learning is immediately seen to be taking place. Children, by social custom, have been conditioned to expect to read and write when they come to school.

After the second or third book is made, the first is often taken home. Some schools keep every book a child makes from the time he enters school until the time he leaves, when he takes them all home. A striking indication of his own mental development is clearly seen by each child.

Early Reading and Writing

The many excellent books on modern Infant teaching methods make it unnecessary for the procedures of early reading and writing to be dealt with here in detail.[2] Such books contain much practical help and suggest procedures along broadly similar lines. Common principles are:

1. Reading and writing are sides of the same coin: progress in both is closely linked.

2. They should both be closely associated with other activities: they are used to record and clarify.

---

[1] L. Hollamby: *Young Children Living and Learning*.

[2] The reader is referred to E. Boyce: *The First Year in School*—E. Hume: *Learning and Teaching in the Infants' School*—E. Mellor: *Education Through Experience in the Infants' School*—N. Goddard: *Reading in the Modern Infants' School*.

Writing has as much importance in the eyes of a child as reading; in some ways it seems to have almost more purpose—certainly it came first historically.

Book making is to be encouraged from the start, although no pressure to read or write should be used. As an interesting activity, both will be available.

Empty books with attractive exteriors or inviting shapes may be on the '5-year-olds' shelf in the writing corner—"My House; My Doll; My Toys" and so on.

Group books should be centred upon the individual and his immediate world: in them pictures will come first. Suitable titles constantly suggest themselves as play and talk proceed. "A Book about Me; About My Holiday; Things I Like; My Dog; A Book about My Mummy and Brothers and Sisters", are just a few examples.

The teacher prepares class books for the children to illustrate by pictures and by writing. "The Children in Our Class; What We Do in School; Where We Live; When I Grow Up; and All things Bright and Beautiful", are a few examples. Sometimes a class book will relate to an activity in which the whole class has taken part, each contributing according to his ability. Here is an example: One Family-grouped class had visited a nearby farm. A model was made; older children made the papiermâché base, painted the background and made farm buildings of cardboard whilst younger children modelled the animals and made fences, trees and bushes. A class book of the farm was made including paintings and drawings by children of all ages. There were pictures of farm animals drawn by the younger children and captioned by the teacher and descriptive writing by the oldest group. It was decorated with patterns and a page of 78 pigs drawn by the youngest group with a description opposite by the oldest children using the words 'seventy-eight' instead of figures. Such books form an excellent addition to the book corner; the teacher rereads them with groups and children read them to each other; strong interest is always shown in "my page".

Scrapbooks, with pictures cut from birthday and Christmas cards, old story books and magazines can be arranged and stuck by the youngest members of the class. They may be captioned by the teacher or by the older children and sometimes by the younger children too. This is an occupation of far greater value than picture and word-matching activities, which bedevil much early reading work. It is the beginning of the classification of knowledge. People, animals, cars, ships, flowers and colours are all sorted into sets. This is in effect a simple form of classification in learning, and a quite advanced stage in the process of intellectual maturation. The first books the 5-year-olds make will be muddled and confused, but slowly experience helps them to see 'classes'.

Reading. Interest meanwhile is being similarly stimulated with appropriate simple books, always available in the book corner. Larger picture books—indeed, all the variety of books which appeal to older children—should be freely available to younger ones also. To say, "You may not use the library corner until you can read," is like saying, "You may not go to the baths until you can swim." If books are desired it is the first step towards wanting to read. There will be reading sessions for the youngest group alone, when a chosen book, a wall story or group book will be the subject of special attention.

Many teachers of Family-grouped classes describe the way in which such sessions send the 5-year-olds to the bookshelves to 'pretend-read' the book which they have enjoyed, or to pore over the pictures. This is a situation difficult to reproduce in a classroom with forty 5-year-olds. In a Family-grouped class the youngest children frequently entice an older child into reading to them. Before long it becomes clear that some children are ready for more positive help.

Reading Readiness and Reading Schemes

No book on Infants' schools is complete without reference to the vexing question of 'Reading Readiness'. It has been the subject of argument for many years and most teachers are familiar with the following ideas:

(a) Children who are required to read too early may fail or succeed only with difficulty, or develop a distaste for reading which can adversely affect learning in general, possibly for the rest of their school life.

(b) Inability to learn to read may have a number of causes. There may be perceptual difficulties (e.g. confusion between similar letters), inadequate vocabulary, partially defective hearing, emotional barriers, or just plain inefficient teaching.

(c) Inability to learn satisfactorily may be connected with rigidity in the use of phonic teaching methods, sentence teaching methods, or both (see the comparatively new ita rational alphabet).[1]

Research[2] indicates that 'reading readiness' depends on a variety of factors, including the following:

1. Physical development, physical maturity of the eyes and development of the organs of speech and hearing.

2. Intellectual development, which is frequently stated in terms of mental age.

3. Development of powers of visual and auditory discrimination.

4. Facility in the association of ideas and problem solving.

5. Social and emotional maturity.

6. The linguistic background of the home.

7. The child's desire to learn to read.

---

[1] For further information see J. Downing: *The Initial Teaching Alphabet.*
[2] A. Sanderson: *A Reexamination of the Idea of Reading Readiness.*

The controversy still continues. It has been fairly continuous for the last thirty years or so, following suggestions by American researchers that a mental age of 6 to 6½ years was the minimum for probable success in reading. Research findings for and against this view continue to be published, and in attempts to devise successful teaching methods there have been many books and reading schemes published.

Teachers' books contain a great deal of wise advice. For instance F. Roe says: "Children are interested in (a) doing things; (b) announcing their doings; (c) learning of other people's doings."

Schonell suggests that the factors involved in reading ability are: (a) level of general ability; (b) special mental abilities (e.g. visual and auditory discrimination of word patterns); (c) experience and language background; (d) emotional attitudes. Schonell favours a mental age of 6 to 6½ years.

Boyce emphasizes: (a) the need for a right attitude to reading; (b) ample opportunity for talking and pre-reading experience; (c) a highly organized and planned programme of cards, games, wall-pictures, graded readers and supplementary books. Most schemes, in fact, have similar highly organized and graded books and materials.

There are many such reading schemes all of which have something of value to offer. In particular the Teacher's Manuals contain helpful advice and no reading scheme should ever be used without studying the appropriate Teacher's Book.

Reading schemes proliferate and research continues, but it is difficult for the practising teacher, who meanwhile has to go on steadily teaching children to read, to thread her way through the maze of 'expert' advice and opinion. A recent study[1] estimates that more than 8,000 studies in the learning and teaching of reading had been published in the last decade!

A strongly worded publication[2] refers to teachers knowing by instinct when children want to learn to read. There is no doubt that 'by instinct' or not, practising teachers know which are the thorniest problems in this controversial subject. Some of their own views follow, with comments.

"Teachers know that in the Infant stages a year's difference in chronological age may encompass other differences of up to four years in different children. Furthermore, apparent abilities may also vary in the same child at different times."

Watts[1] discusses reading readiness in relation to intelligent and dull children, and also in relation to dull children from good homes. He suggests starting reading at 5½ to 6 years, placing emphasis on the *desire* of children to read. He says: "It is when children see grownups

---

[1] J. C. Daniels and H. Diack: *Progress in Reading.*
[2] A. Sanderson: *A Reexamination of the Idea of Reading Readiness.*

actually getting value from reading that they themselves want to read." Such a comment is particularly pertinent to the Family-grouped classroom as here the younger or more immature children see not only the adult, but other children getting pleasure and value from books.

"Not all children learn in the same way. Some seem to like phonics whilst others may make rapid progress with 'look and say'."

This is in accord with a study by Wheeler who considers that children tend "to fall into two groups according to their characteristic mode of reasoning . . . one being analytic or explicit reasoning, proceeding by a succession of logical steps; the other an implicit or synthetic apperception . . . resulting from a kind of comprehensive insight".[2]

This does not mean that all children should be subjected to a double battery of reading teaching (sentence and phonic together), certainly not at first. But it does indicate that a variety of simple books and readers should be available so a child may take to the one which suits him best, and that the approach of the teacher must be completely flexible.

"When there is plenty of attractive reading material, in a relaxed atmosphere, children take to it naturally."

This also is in accord with the view of researchers. The Education Research Re-examination speaks of the need for a "mildly provocative pre-reading experience" and says: "reading is a skill which occurs only in an advanced culture, and in an environment which demands it."[3]

Once again the Family-grouped environment is particularly valuable. Here is not an adult requiring 40 non-readers to come to grips with early reading difficulties, but other children at various stages of success, visibly facing up to problems in acquiring this desirable skill, practising with teacher's help and finally succeeding, with every evidence of enjoyment. The incentive is an immediate one.

Downing refers to a study of nearly 50 children who learnt to read between the ages of 3 and 5, and remarks: "The help of parents and siblings appeared to have been an important factor in their early development of reading ability."[4] In a Vertically Age-grouped class it might almost be said that the successful readers take the place of parents and siblings. It is a common sight in such a classroom to see one or more of the younger children coming voluntarily to listen to older ones as they read to the teacher, leaning against her as she sits, or looking over an older child's book. Here learning is indeed "caught, not taught".

---

[1] A. Watts: *The Language and Mental Development of the Child.*
[2] Described by E. Churchill: *Counting and Measuring in the Infants' School.*
[3] A. Sanderson: *A Reexamination of the Idea of Reading Readiness.*
[4] J. Downing: *Is a Mental Age of Six Essential for Reading Readiness?*

There is reference in some of the research literature[1] to the earliest age at which children *can* learn to read. Cases are cited of children reading at $2\frac{1}{2}$ or 3 years of age. As the anxiety about getting children to read is so widespread amongst teachers and parents, and allegations concerning illiteracy are frequently made, it is appropriate to ask, "Just what is the purpose of demonstrating that children can, under certain circumstances, be taught to read when very young?" It poses the question, "Should we if we could?"

A pertinent point seldom referred to—perhaps *the* most pertinent point—is that reading is the key to *second-hand* experience and knowledge. Books are indispensable, but it is better that they become indispensable to children only after they have acquired first-hand knowledge and experience which books can then extend and illumine. Toddlers of 2 years old should be moving, prattling, listening, touching, investigating and manipulating: reading can wait. It is significant that in at least two cases where very early reading learning (2·0 years and 2·9 years) occurred, after a while both children "became resistant to further learning" and it was temporarily discontinued.

It is clear that high-pressure methods, be they phonic, sentence, ita, or other, can achieve reading results at an early age. But we are not so much concerned with whether children are reading at 5 years, but with what (if anything) they are reading voluntarily at 15 or even 25 years.[2] Learning to read is more than an end in itself, and of this we are reminded when we hear of children being unwisely transferred to the Junior school while still unready for the 'formal approach' in reading[3]; that is, for practising reading as a skill apart from using it in connection with other activities.

Teachers and researchers are unanimous on one issue—positive psychological injury results from forcing a child to read too soon. The difficulty lies in determining when 'too soon' may be, bearing in mind the "injustice of being compelled to postpone reading beyond the point of readiness".

In a Vertically Age-grouped classroom, with reading at various levels going on all the time, and books of all kinds freely available, it is not likely that any child will be left 'too late', and in fact, any child can start at almost any moment of any day. The advantages are plain.

The final point of importance upon which teachers seem to agree is this: "*If a child is left to follow his natural inclination to read he is likely, when he does start, to make rapid progress and experience success: both are vitally important.*"

---

[1] R. Lynn: *Reading Readiness and the Perceptual Abilities of Young Children.*

[2] See A. Hughes: *Education and the Democratic Ideal* for a discussion of the idea of 'functional illiteracy'.

[3] H. James and others: *Periods of Stress in the Primary School.*

Books and Reading Practice

The reading corner in the Family-grouped classroom should hold a wide variety of books, large and small, picture and story, from one-sentence-one-picture books of a very elementary kind, to story books, reference books, picture dictionaries and simple encyclopaedias. Children will also have access to a stock of story and reference books in the Infants' School Library: each school has its own way of arranging this. Some schools differentiate the 'learning to read' books from others, but in most schools all kinds are freely available.

A particularly successful scheme in one Family-grouped school is that of sorting and arranging the graded readers into separate painted boxes, each section being known by a different colour; the 'yellow library' and the 'blue library' and so on. Each box contains books of approximately the same reading level. The first books are shórt and easy; the children (after considerable pre-reading experience) quickly read through them, and each reinforces the other. Second and following stages are similarly planned.

Thus rapid increase in vocabulary, ideas, sentence construction and in the sizes of the successive books, which so frequently deters a child who is working steadily through the grades of any one scheme, is avoided, and the children are more likely to be continuously successful. Each child keeps his own record, ticking off the books read on a manila card of appropriate colour.

There are children who do no need this orderly progression from book to book, and who find it irksome. They prefer to tackle a really difficult (more mature) book, or find their way by means of the pictures in which they are interested. It would be unwise in such a case to say, "You have not read such -and-such a book, so you cannot go on."

Discussing the repetition of unsuccessful experience, Wall observes: "It is also questionable whether in all, or most aspects of the curriculum, primary or secondary, the mastery of one stage is an essential factor in progress at the next. The logical progression of the development of a subject like mathematics *may* correspond with the psychological progression of learning, and commonsense appears to lend some support to the notion. But even with such a subject, in the absence of adequate research on the way in which concepts are formed, one can be by no means sure . . . In acquiring skills like reading, and composition in the mother tongue, it seems likely that factors of intellectual and emotional maturity, freshness and variety of experience are more important than exposure to supposedly logical learning sequences derived from the subject itself."[1]

Once interested in reading, children enjoy practice as they do with other new skills, and frequently ask to "be heard". This vital stage of reading-learning imposes a great strain on the teacher of the Tradi-

---

[1] W. Wall, F. Schonell, C. Olson: *Failure in School.*

tionally-grouped 6-year-old class where this interest usually blossoms, since she knows that the children can sustain little effort on their own and need much encouragement and help.

Many teachers fall back on 'reading occupations' for those not being heard. It is difficult to be sure that these are all purposeful and interesting to all children. Apparatus of the picture-word matching variety is useless unless it is checked when the children have done it. If it is found incorrect, this means a teaching session perhaps with only one child, which is time-consuming and may not be valuable unless followed up.

Hollamby[1] has a useful discussion on the making of reading apparatus; along with helpful suggestions, she comments that apparatus should not be made "in a vacuum" but arise from the immediate need of a child and be written before his eyes. This would only be possible for a small number of children at a time.

On the whole, teachers of Family-grouped classes use little 'practice' of this kind. Practice related to reading-learning more often takes the form of writing and creative activity. For instance, a group of individuals might each be making pages for a House Book, or one on "My Toys", words needed being looked up in the spelling corner, or obtained with help from an older child. A teaching session on phonics may lead to children searching out their own lists of words beginning with certain letters, or containing certain combinations. At this stage, children are often really interested in words. Such activity, freely chosen, gives as much pleasure as using muscular skill, or painting and sewing.

A few moments spent on flashcards may end in the group going away to a corner and practising with each other, each taking turns to be teacher: older children often enjoy the chance to organize this kind of work, and their own learning is reinforced.

Reading and Writing Inspired by Interests

The reading and writing work which stems from other activities is the most popular and rewarding type of 'practice' possible. For twenty or more years, books on Infant teaching methods have described such work. One or two examples are here condensed from such books.

Simpson: *Creative Work in the Infants' School*

Starting-point: Discussion between class-teacher and intelligent children on starting a class newspaper.

Development: Voting for editor and committee; delegation of responsibility for news items, nature news, stories, poems and riddles; creation of newspaper office; posters; letters to the editor; reading of the class newspaper in the library by means of a ticket purchased for 3d. (Who can say where play ends and work begins?)

[1] L. Hollamby: *Young Children Living and Learning.*

Goddard: *Reading in the Modern Infants' School*
Starting point: Hospital play following on children's own experiences.
Development: Hospital equipment of every kind; notices telling
   patients where to go and what to do; labels for people (nurses,
   doctors) and for patients' ailments; labels for equipment and
   medicine; wall story and vocabulary list.

Hollamby, in *Young Children Living and Learning*, describes an
interest beginning with the Post Office extending to foreign lands and
collections of foreign stamps. One teacher however saw the essential
need of children to *visit* a Post Office, and pointed out that young
children rarely enter one, seldom buy stamps, and never have occasion to post parcels. When they have seen and done these things
themselves, interest is very lively indeed, and letter writing within the
classroom becomes more significant.

Hollamby: *Young Children Living and Learning*
Starting point: A child making a wooden aeroplane.
Development: Play flights to other countries; maps and the globe;
   growth of a 'travel agency'; passports (measuring for height);
   single and return fares; flight crash (doctors, nurses, air-crew); air-
   hostess's note-book and an extension of interest into France and the
   French language.

Such work/play is a lively amalgam of fantasy and imaginative
play, children's intellectual activity, and the teacher's experience and
knowledge. It would be hard to say where one ends and the other
begins. It is equally difficult to predict what direction an interest will
take, and it is necessary for the vitality of the activity that the children's own involvement should be the driving force behind it, and not
the teacher's pre-prepared plans or dominating influence. But a
teacher will often see possibilities which unfold only gradually to the
children as they play and work.
   Teachers unfamiliar with the organization of active learning of this
kind do not always appreciate clearly how such individual or group
work gets under way.

Starting points
   Possible starting points are listed below, and these are followed by
examples of recent work in Family-grouped classes:
   Children's play revealing a special interest may (not must) be taken
further with help from the teacher.
   Some item or object of interest brought to school by a child. For an
example see the study of prehistoric animals described on page 92.
   A stimulating object brought in by the teacher. For an example see
the description of train building on page 94.

A new book shown by teacher or child. For an example see the work on clocks described on page 95.

A visitor to the class. Examples of people whose personal descriptions of experiences or daily work interest children are: *The school nurse*. She can describe things suitable for the hospital interest referred to on page 90. *The school cook*. A teacher describes the strong interest which her children developed in food and food values after a tour of the school kitchen. They learned about quantities and measurements normally outside their experience. 'Gallons' took on a new meaning. *The Schoolkeeper*. One talked to the children about his equipment (brooms, mops and pails) and the children took more interest in keeping the playground tidy. *Children's parents*. These may be train drivers, shopkeepers, postmen, footballers or librarians.

Special occasions, such as Christmas, Harvest Festival and so on. One school always has a celebration, with a display of children's work on the school's 'birthday'.[1]

Visits to places of interest. These may be starting points or part of the development of an interest. Teachers are constantly amazed to discover the paucity of children's knowledge of their own environment. Children living in towns often go no further than the nearest row of shops. Of nearby railway stations, bus garages, fire stations, libraries, statues, rivers, bridges and so on they have virtually no experience. Their knowledge of the layout of local streets is scant and they often cannot say where the nearest pillar-box is, or what kind of trees grow in the nearby park. Village children are frequently ignorant about their own churches, farms, ponds and routes to nearby towns and the towns themselves.

All this and much more is experience which could be opened up to Infants. A teacher described part of the interesting work which followed a visit to the zoo. Children made wire and paper animals; books about animals were written and the class-teacher made a large map of the world and the children stuck into it small flags indicating which part of the world the animals came from. The children (5 to 7 years) each made contributions appropriate to their age and ability, some only painting and modelling, others writing and looking up facts (e.g. What does a kangaroo like to eat?).

Teachers experienced in these methods stress the fact that children's pleasure in their play or experience will evaporate if, in her anxiety, a teacher tries to over-exploit the lead-in to academic work. An enthusiast for 'activity methods' described how a child, showing a boat which he had made, said, "I've drawn it, measured it and written about it. What shall I do next?" Whereupon a sceptic was heard to mutter, "I know what I'd say—*play with it!!*"

---

[1] For a very moving account of a special Christmas celebration in a village school see S. Marshall: *An Experiment in Education.*

Play is satisfying in itself and does not always need a follow-through; children should not always be asked to write about their experiences. A country walk or a visit to the zoo should be followed by plenty of talk and, if the children wish, by expression of interest through drawing, handwork or painting. They will often say, "We could make that," or ask a question which will lead the teacher to say, "Let's look it up." Children need to soak themselves in experience, or perhaps be allowed a fallow period before doing further work. Many teachers report a return to an interest perhaps a month or even a term later.

An experienced headteacher summarized these principles by remarking, "You cannot expect rich language to come from scant experience." Examples follow of combined language and interest work from Family-grouped classes.

A Study of Prehistoric Animals

Starting point: Asked to choose a book for the teacher to read a boy chose a book on prehistoric animals.

Development: Some children began to make prehistoric animals in plasticine and clay.

The teacher then showed them how to make better models with wire, paste and paper; these were painted and varnished. Enthusiasm began to grow. A large model was set up, the base being made of pasted paper over boxes and a realistic swamp was created with mashed-up egg boxes. All the children now drew a picture for a class book and the teacher wrote the captions. The older children began to draw and write for themselves and some did several pieces of writing. More books were consulted.

The local library was visited, books were borrowed and used for making more accurate models and spellings were looked up. Reference books were brought from home, and one child's brother drew a picture for the class book at home.

By now all the children were involved, and work was going on all day. Language, both spoken and written, was vivid, and the children used casually, and with correct pronunciation, the difficult names of the various creatures—dinosaur, brontosaurus, ichthyosaurus, diplodocus and stegosaurus.

The older children were taken to the Natural History Museum in Kensington; this was quite a long and complex journey and meant being out all day and taking lunch. It was the farthest distance that most of the children had travelled (they came from a school in a poor area) and it was a great occasion. Some of them were awestruck, some excited and some practical. One 7-year-old girl (with a reading age of 11 years 6 months) read all the notices under the exhibits. Notes were made of the lengths of some of the skeletons, and on return to school the classroom and hall were measured to see how the brontosaurus would 'fit in'. The children came to the conclusion that if the tail were chopped off, it would just fit into the width of the hall.

Two special points of interest were: (a) in the words of the teacher, "some of the children really developed an enthusiasm for books. For the first time they really looked into them to obtain the information they wanted, and to check the accuracy of their models"; (b) even the 5-year-olds were infected by the interest and enthusiasm. A visitor to the classroom noted it was a small, babyish looking 5-year-old boy who brought her different models to look at, naming them correctly and stating which children had made them. Two terms later the same child led another visitor to the book corner and showed her the book on prehistoric animals, giving her a detailed account of each animal as he turned the pages. Towards the end of the term another 5-year-old boy brought to school some small models of prehistoric animals and persuaded some older children to help him make a miniature swamp.

An example of children's writing in connection with this work taken from "The Second Book of Prehistoric Animals" follows. Each piece of writing followed a picture. The first example is by Victor, aged 7 years 9 months:

"My Dinosaur is As Big as Ten elephants. He is grey. He does look fierce. He is A plant-eater. The Dinosaurs are dead now But in the museums you can see the bones of them The stegosaurus protect himself from his enimyies with his bony plates he is a plant eater."

It happened that at another Family-grouped school another boy was taking a particular interest in prehistoric animals. Some of his free writing is included as an example of the quality of writing which young children can produce when following their own interests. This was written by Guy, aged 7 years 9 months:

"Once upon a time when the earth was young there were years called the age of reptiles . . . But these reptiles were not lizards and other common liveing things that live-to-day. there were things called tyreldactals and Allosaurus and Brontosaurus and Diplodocus. these reptiles lived hundred and milleons of years ago. there were meat-eating dinosaurs and plant-eating things. when you go to a museom you see these reptiles bones. there are reptiles called ankylosaurus and iriccraptops and analosaurus and stegosauras. stegosaurus has big sharp spikes like amour for deefending hiself. So has ankylosauras. Anatosaurus has a sort of duck-bill. the shape of there mouth made it almost inposerble for them to eat. corythosaurus was a swimmer—really I belive that he was a very good swimmer. Tyrannosaurus-rex walked on big black legs and has little arms. camptosaurus has a sort of pinted (pointed) scull and thin neck. at the end of preyostoric animals there were mamales that most probely eat dinosaurs eggs. Brachiosaurus lives in South Americer some of these animals were great fighters and great runners. But Nowerdays it is better than the age of the reptiles, because some of man-eating dinosaur's could eat us. so that's why Nowerdays is better than the age of reptiles do you see what I mean. Strathiomimas was very very very little."

Guy made vivid drawings illustrated by captions:

"Ankylosaurus had a hard bone on his tail so he could deal with donosaur's by ckrushing them."

"This mamel rakes round for dinosaur's eggs."

"This is the dinosaur's egg being eaten."

"Tyreldactels have long sharp dager's on the ball of there scull. Stregobaurus was a great fighter. You see when another animal came to kill it—it broke it teeth. there were swamps in those day's some animals got caught in them. But then these things died-out dinosaur's fishe's tortesses mamals died-out   Sort of crabs died out the whole world of dinosaurs and preystoric animals were dead."

An Interest in Transport

Starting point: The teacher brought a large cylindrical cardboard drum, which was about 20 inches long and 7 inches in diameter. It was immediately taken by a boy who announced that he would make a train. He had seen 'Stephenson's Rocket' in a picture book and decided his train was to be this.

Development: The 'Rocket' was made and variously described in writing as "George Stephenson's engine" and "Stephenson's loco-motive".

The interest began to spread into other forms of locomotion, and other children made models of boats, aeroplanes, airships and balloons. A book with pictures and written work included descriptions of olden-day rafts, boats, the *Queen Mary*, balloons, airships, a horse, the "iron horse", one of the "first trains", and aeroplanes. An ingenious way of making airships and balloons was developed, by winding pasted paper strips around blow-up rubber balloons.

An example of writing which accompanied pictures:

"Wilber and Orville made the first airoplane. It is old fashioned now and people do not use them. They have double wings and people travelled on them. They thought it was wonderful."

An Interest in Clocks

Starting point: The teacher read to a group of children a *Junior True Book* called "Telling the Time".[1]

Development: The children promptly began to explore ways of telling the time other than with the familiar clock.

---

[1] *Junior True Book Series*—Frederick Muller Ltd.

Interest waned after a short time, but was revived following a power failure in the district, when several children brought candles to school. They experimented with candle-clocks, and went on to read and write about egg-timers, sundials, shadow-sticks and water clocks. Later they were further stimulated by seeing examples of water clocks and candle-clocks in the Children's Gallery of the Science Museum in South Kensington. Extracts from captions in the "Clock Book" are:

"The grandfather clock goes tick, tock, tock, but when the big grandfather clock strikes twelve o'clock everybody goes to bed."

"My Mum has an alarm clock, and the alarm clock wakes my Mum up every morning."

"The sundial is much like a shadow stick. If the sun is not shining you cannot tell the time."

"This is a wrist-watch my Dad had a wrist watch my Dad carries his wrist watch everywhere he goes."

A Model of the School

Starting point: The children had been cutting cardboard boxes and cartons to use the cardboard flat, but the teacher showed them ways of using the actual boxes. First 'rooms' were made, then a garage, then a large model of the school.

Development: Three boys initially began the interest but others were drawn in to help. The model included 6 classrooms, the hall, the vestibule, the outside playground, terraces, the library, kitchen, dining hall, staffroom and so on.

Investigations were made into sizes and shapes—rooms and corridors were stepped out and windows counted.

The purpose of each part of the school was investigated, and the work of the people in it. A considerable amount of written work evolved and was mounted in a large book, which was also freely illustrated. When the model became too large for the classroom, it was placed first in the corridor (the children made notices saying, "Please do not touch"), then in the hall. The work continued for a period of two terms and into the third. The class-teacher said, "I began to get rather tired of it, and thought the children would too. But they didn't. They kept me at it." Examples of writing from the "Book of the School":

"Today I made the hall doors and I stuck them on the hall and it looks nice now it is on."

"We had to go in the hall and have a look at it and draw them and it takes a long time if you want to do it nicely."

"Today I had to mix red for one side of the hall and I got a cup and got a spoon and put a bit of light red and dark red in the cup and a brounea (browny) yellow. Then I put some water in it and sterd it up and *I went to the hall and looked to see if it was the right couler* and it was so I brallt the paint back to the clasroom and painted the side of the hall."

Note the solving of a problem in the practical situation (checking and testing). Such situations crop up over and over again in work of this kind.

"I went to the kitchen and asked the lady how many cooks there were and the lady said 12 and me and Paula said what do you do and the lady said I wash up. 1 supervisor 5 assistant cooks 2 servers 2 lay the tables."

"Mrs Robbins cleans the school and some other ladys and they have to have a bucket to clean the floor and broom and they do it when all the children have gonee x gone home."

In all the examples given "the technical processes of learning to read and write fall into their proper places as aids to recording and communicating . . . the children grow eager to master these tools."[1]

Routine Work: Using Books

Vital and interesting as the foregoing type of work is, it does not occupy all children all of the time. There are also times when children look to the teacher for guidance in more routine work.

Children will still need periods of reading practice, either as individuals, in pairs, or occasionally in groups. The teacher may read all, or part of a new book to them and then hand it to the children to complete or enjoy. Reading for pleasure should infect every child; the teacher's own pleasure in books will certainly be reflected in the class.

As the children grow increasingly fluent, it becomes evident that there are many ways of using books. There is 'reading for pleasure' as suggested above, which usually means the reading of a whole book; there is 'dipping in' and finding out what a book is about with possibly a decision whether to read it or not; there is 'part reading' or selecting parts of books for information or instruction and partial reading of collections of short stories or poems; and there is 'finding out' or going to a book with a definite purpose to find out specific facts.

All these ways of using books should be part of a child's experience: not having to "read this one right through before you can have another".

Apart from the use of books in connection with a special interest, teachers have devised many ways of sending quite young children to books for 'finding out' purposes, and such devices should be part of the environment available. Examples are:

1. Cards or booklets giving such instructions as, "Find a story about a cat—draw him and write his name." The difference should be noted between this and setting children to write answers to questions

---

[1] S. Isaacs: *Intellectual Growth in Young Children.*

The *Prehistoric Monster* project (*see* page 92). *An extract from the class book and the model built by the children*

Self-organized music-making. The boy at the back of the picture is "announcing" into a microphone

on a set passage. Initiative is required and the children may make a choice of a card or exercise which appeals to them.

There may be a direction to a special book such as, "Look in the *Observers' Book of Birds* and find two birds with short legs, and two with long legs. Draw them and write their names and say what kind of food they eat. Or "Look in the *Golden Book of Ships*. Draw and write down three different ways of making a boat go along."

2. Some teachers encourage children to use 'Assignments of work'. Such work is only suitable for children who have mastered the techniques of reading and writing and can organize part of their working day. But such children seem to derive the same satisfaction and pleasure from these self-organized tasks as they do from periods of pure play. The last term of their Infants' school year is often a time for enjoying this method of working. Children should not be expected to undertake it before they can do it with real pleasure.

One skilled headteacher has prepared a series of booklets on various themes such as: animals, the sky, homes and houses, trains. Each booklet contains suggestions for something to read, something to write and something to do. Each section is printed in a different colour, which is retained throughout the series. These are very popular and have provided the stimulus for reading and written work of a high standard.

Another teacher has prepared several series of small booklets (of various colours to denote the level of difficulty) in which written work is based on the investigation of a subject through reading certain books, e.g. the *How—Why—Where Books* by Arnold or the series, *Light, Water, Magnets, Heat, Sound,* by Basil Blackwell. Having read the appropriate book, the children make their own book, with free writing and profuse illustration. Pictures, still the child's most natural means of expression, come first.

Of the purpose of reading, Sealey and Gibbon say: "It is one of the functions of the Junior school to wean children away from the adult as a source of information."[1] Infants' schools in which work such as described occurs are certainly anticipating this function of the Junior school, and because the activity is based on the choice of the child, there is no fear of his interest in 'finding out' becoming stale.

Books or cards of instruction are very popular. They can be a source of new ideas to children, and very useful practice in paying close attention to text. They are of far greater value than exercises of the traditional question-and-answer type, or filling in blanks in sentences, because the child can see for himself, by the result he achieves, whether he has followed the instructions correctly.

Examples are books or cards prepared by teachers of: simple knit-

---

[1] L. Sealey and V. Gibbon: *Communication and Learning in the Infants' School.*

ting patterns, easy directions for making dolls' clothes, simple cooking recipes or instructions for simple science experiments. Others may have questions on the cards, such as: "Find out what happens when . . . (e.g. you put a cork or a nail in water)."

Comics, children's books and annuals often contain suitably simple but interesting sets of instructions which can be cut out and mounted.

These devices cannot take the place of the children's own free and self-initiated creative work, but have a value in training children to find out for themselves how to do things they want to do. The teacher becomes one of the sources, rather than the only source, of information and help.

There are books that, although intended for adults or older children, young children in many classrooms use with enthusiasm and success. Examples are, Sayers: *Let's Make Something* and Klein: *Animals to Fold*.

One 7-year-old boy worked steadily, without stopping, for some weeks, through the second of these books, managing eventually to follow instructions and build models which an adult would find taxing. He announced to a visitor who was admiring his assembled handiwork, "This is the one I couldn't do," and indicated in the book one very complicated creature. "But I will one day," he added. It was an extraordinary example of sustained interest and effort. Meeting a difficulty had not disheartened this child: from his own self-initiated experience he had developed confidence which with further effort would overcome the difficulty. He had understood what he was doing and had in some cases taught other children who had become interested. He had found his own way to this interest—but his teacher had made it available.

Free Writing

In one sense all the written work described above is free; that is, it is not teacher-directed, and is closely linked with freely chosen pursuits. There are, however, some children who enjoy written language for its own sake; for them it is a medium of self-expression as natural as painting, clay or drama and movement. When the shackles of formality are struck off, a wonderful sense of freedom and release gives vitality to children's writing. Children for whom it is a natural mode of expression write freely, without fear of reproof or correction of spelling or grammar. Their outpouring of uninhibited language is very different from the stilted sentences copied by the whole class, which we formerly associated with Infants' writing. They may have help, but their writing is not interfered with.

As a result their writing is vigorous and imaginative, coming directly from school lives of interesting content: from poems and stories of good quality; from encouragement of spoken thought and personal involvement in the writing. For all children the needs are the same—play, talk, stimulating experience, drawing, writing, reading, and conversation, with literature of beauty and vitality introduced by the teacher.

Some children come to writing as a means of expression very quickly and easily. Here are some examples of fluent free writing from Family-grouped classrooms. The first is by Rosemary, aged 7 years; it is called "The Magic glufs (gloves)".

"Once upon a time ther lived a little girl and this little girl had a pear of Magic glufs and the glufs were red and the pear of glufs cood x could speak and the pear of glufs said to the little girl will you get me some food and the little girl wandered who it was and the pear of glufs said it is your Magic pear of glufs so the little girl got the Magic pear of glufs some food and the pear of glufs eat it all up and the Magic Glufs said you can have a wish and the little girl wished that she could have a silver dress and her wish came tror and she cepd her glufs all the time."

The second example is an extract from "The Winter Olympic Games 1964" by David, aged 7 years 2 months:

"The Olympic games are held in Innsbruck in Austria. There is plenty of snow in the mountains for the skiers. They face down the mountains on skis. They have competitions from jumping on skis. When they jump on skis it makes you think that they are flying. There will be tobogganing for the first tim in the Olympic games. The tobogganning men are now allowed to lie down. the toboggans can go about 60 m.p.h."

David's work filled a small book; it was illustrated, and concluded with a chart showing the number of gold, silver and bronze medals awarded to fourteen different countries.

Note the intense satisfaction Margaret (6 years 6 months) is shown to be getting from school in this next example:

"One day a little boy and girl started school. They were ownley 4 years old but they like it very much. Darrol and Vanita had started a week beefor the little girl and boy who's names where Desmond and Karen they liked the Wendy House the best they played with the dolls house they read books they sang songs and dressed up and played in the playground and then they had their dinner and after dinner they wrote a story about school after school they told there mummy all about school."

Another example from a book of stories written by 7-year-olds on the idea of "One Dark Night":

"It was a cold dark night and everything was quiet when suddenly there come a big loud scratching sound and it came louder and louder util you saw it and it was a big big fat spider and it was scratching his face and it said I am hungry and if everything is quiet and dark I will look for something to eat so off he went and he said I will catch that big fly and her 9 baby flys so he jumped up to catch them and he eat the flys and then this spider said to himself why can't I have some baby spiders and the fly that the spider had eaten said you are a daddy spider so there."

Although such children seldom need to be given a starting-point there are occasions when they say, "What shall I write?"

Teachers' devices for dealing with this question include:

1. A large book labelled, "What Shall I Write About?", each page with a suggestion or stimulus of some kind. Perhaps a piece of blue velvet ribbon, some white fur in cellophane, a coloured feather, a picture of a horse or mouse, a painted pattern of mosaic shapes, a bud, a single word or sentence, and so on.

2. A 'treasure chest' of oddments into which a child may dip. This could contain any of the small objects which strike a child's fancy. A little bell, models of cars, animals or people, a baby's shoe, a plastic spoon, marbles, a row of beads or a large safety pin are all good examples. Once this 'chest' has begun, all is grist to the teacher's mill. A short walk around Woolworths will yield a collection of little 'treasures' and children will bring their own objects to put in it.

3. Starting a story, either orally or in writing, which children may finish. "Once upon a time a little tree grew in a wood . . ." or "Once a little boy climbed into an aeroplane . . ."

4. Reading a poem.

5. Group ideas, in which an adventure, funny names, noises, smells or feelings of different kinds are discussed. The essence of such talking together is that the group should be small, all involved in the talk, and the language evocative. This is use of language at a fairly sophisticated level, to be reserved for those intellectually mature enough for it. There are many such children nearing the end of Infants' school life, and teachers are often at a loss to know how best to help them to go on growing intellectually.

No matter what the starting point may be, children's work often shows an element of emotional release in dealing with feelings of fear or distress. The following two examples are taken almost at random from the work in one school. The first was written by Carol (6 years 3 months) around a picture supplied by the teacher:

"Micky was a dog and one day he was having a walk in the garden and the gate was opne and he ran out of the gate. He ran down the road he hid himself in a bush he ran away he ran so far away he lost him self he barked and barked but he was still lost. He walked away but he was lost now he was afraid. He went on and he found a farm he went to the hens he found seven eggs in the nest. He sniffed them and looked at the hens and the hens looked at him and said chick chick and he said bark bark bark. The hens ran over the farm and Mick chased them Mick ran so fast that he ran right past them so the hens ran in to the nest. Mick ran out of the farm Mick that (thought) that he was horrible. He walked up the road and he bumped in to some body so the man walked a away and Mick went away too. He walked away very slowly. The farmer was a horrible man. He kept hitting him and Mick didn't like him. He went on feeling sad because it was nearly night. He ran and ran but it was still getting dark. He hid behind a bush to try to keep himself warm. He hid so nobody would see him cars went by.

He ran away he wished he hadn't run away. He still ran he ran so far that he could see his house. He ran towards it and was safely at home."

The second example came after a little boy had drawn a free picture of jungle animals:

"Once there was an elephant. He lived in the jungool and his feet shook the jungool. Here was a parrot was up in a tree. He thought the elephant had a bad skin and he larfed at him and tiger came and the tiger lafd at him. He sed he needed exasis. And the elephant had some exasis and his skin was beter."

Spelling Help

Reference has been made to writing freely without fear of reproof or correction of spelling or grammar. Should spelling errors never be corrected: should incorrect grammar (Tommy and me went) always be ignored? And if not, will not incorrect spelling and grammar become firmly established?

The first aim of language work in the Infants' school is the speaking and writing of vivid, fluent English. If fluency is sacrificed to spelling and grammar, it may never be recaptured: children will then be left with the ability to spell and write correctly, and no desire to use it. The first essential is to have something to say, the next to be unafraid to say it.

Children become wary of using the expressive or interesting word which presents difficulty in spelling if they are torn between spelling the word wrongly and finding a red slash on their work, and stopping the flow of thought to find out how to spell the word. Rejection of both writing and spelling is likely to result.

Caught in the urgent flow of their writing, children often spell or write incorrectly words and phrases which they can manage quite correctly in less intense moments. Such passages or words will often be corrected later by the children themselves when they read aloud or rewrite a fair copy, perhaps for a class magazine or newspaper.

The above principles emerge from teachers' discussion of the matter, as do the following:

1. Help should always be available if the children want it, but they should not feel pressured either by overt or covert criticism by the teacher.

2. Early familiarity with the names of letters of the alphabet is useful; i.e. rote learning of the alphabet. "Many children enjoy learning the alphabet and recognizing letters by name."[1] Such teaching is often done at home.

3. Individual 'word books' in alphabetical order should be provided as soon as the children show signs of wanting to write; in them teachers write any word which is specially asked for, or children enter any word which strikes their fancy. "My Word Book" should be a source of pride and interest, and the teacher should show actively that it is valued.

4. Picture dictionaries, word books, word cards and lists (people, colours, days of the week, places and so on) should be easily available in the writing corner and the children encouraged to know about them. The teacher should add words which she finds the children spell incorrectly, and draw attention to the fact.[2]

5. Phonic teaching is part of the programme of learning to read. Generally, it will begin towards the middle of the last year of Infants' school, when reading has first been mastered by the 'look and say' method, and phonics are added to help children deal with unfamiliar words. Children to whom phonic work makes a special appeal may join in such learning groups at any age.

6. Word occupations (see page 89) and word games such as I Spy, The Parson's Cat (oral) and Scrabble have a place as pastimes with a group or with the class.

7. There should be a basic principle of not 'marking' the children's work (i.e. of not giving a mark such as 'good work' or a tick). Encouragement and interest by written comment: "I like this story", or, "What happened to the princess after all?" is better. "Tell me about your friends", or, "Who came to your party?" will be a much better stimulus to further writing than "Not enough" or even "very good".

Corrections, stars, and ticks indicate little personal interest by the teacher and may evoke disappointment or jealousy. There should be a tacit assumption that a child is always doing the best he can, and his work is worthwhile for its own sake; that he does not work for a tick or star from the teacher.

Vicars Bell, speaking of the importance of children not becoming 'pen-shy', suggests teachers should not, "during the child's early

---

[1] H.M.S.O.: *Some Suggestions for Teachers of English and Others in Primary and Secondary Schools and in Further Education.*

[2] For special help with the question of Infants' spelling see N. Goddard: *Reading in the Modern Infants' School.*

stages, be impatient for improvement" and testifies that the foresight and patience with which teachers accept work of "ostensibly lower standard" is rewarded ultimately by rapid progress to the writing of lively, accurate English.[1]

Handwriting

A number of varied approaches exist towards helping children to write efficiently. The skill is a complex one and children's eyes, hand-eye coordination and muscular control vary greatly.

There are teachers who consider writing skill is best acquired by teaching children simple print script; others prefer to teach the beginnings of italic script; others train children to join letters in a simple running hand from the start. These are the three main variations: the choice is a matter of personal taste and school policy.

However, certain basic ideas emerge which are common to all these methods. Suggestions made by teachers are:

1. Plenty of drawing, painting and modelling strengthens finger, hand and arm muscles and improves eye-hand coordination often better than actual writing practice.

2. Writing achievement may not be related to chronological age; a small girl, for instance, often has a standard of neat precise work which is impossible for an older, large boy whose muscle coordination is less efficient. Eyes also undergo maturational changes and at about 6 years many children are rather long-sighted.

3. Copying from the board is a strain; it should never be arranged so that a child has to turn and twist his body to look at the board. Ideally the teacher's written work should be immediately to hand so that children can copy or trace without frequent re-focusing.

4. It should be the accepted practice for children needing to look up spelling, to be free to go right up to the spelling book or corner to copy.

5. Materials must be a help, not a hindrance. Thick pencils and stubby wax crayons are needed by many children long after others are able to discard them for something finer: they should always be available. Lined paper presents another difficulty with the need to make a letter a specific size. Children's natural handwriting size varies as does that of adults. They learn to write admirably on blank paper, and need thereafter never take to lines. Large blank sheets of paper, which can be decorated or illustrated, enable a piece of work to be seen as a whole: every child should have the chance to produce such pieces of work because there is then some point in practising.

6. Handwriting practice is easy to arrange: there are many varieties of handwriting cards and books from which teachers can make a

---

[1] V. Bell: *On Learning the English Tongue.*

choice. Tracing and copying should be pleasurable and relaxing tasks which children undertake because they know it will help them to write better.

7. Handwriting is the servant of language, and exists to store and communicate thought. It is important that it should do so effectively (be quick to write, clear and easily read), but its value is always secondary to the ideas it transmits.

Understanding Number

The early part of this Chapter laid stress on the importance of cultivating fluency in speech: plenty of talk is also essential to the satisfactory mastery of number ideas.

The language of number in its specific sense is not easy to structure, partly because many of the words are used in a general sense also. Consider the following passage from *Alice Through the Looking Glass*:

"She can't do addition," the Queen interrupted. "Can you do subtraction? Take nine from eight."

"Nine from eight I can't you know," Alice replied very readily, "but——"

"She can't do subtraction," said the White Queen. "Can you do division? Divide a loaf by a knife—what's the answer to that?"

"I suppose——" Alice was beginning, but the Red Queen answered for her. "Bread and butter, of course. Try another subtraction sum. Take a bone from a dog. What remains?"

Alice considered. "The bone wouldn't remain, of course, if I took it—and the dog wouldn't remain; it would come to bite me—and I'm sure I shouldn't remain!"

"Then you think nothing would remain?" said the Red Queen.

"I think that's the answer."

"Wrong, as usual," said the Red Queen: "the dog's temper would remain."

"But I don't see how——"

"Why, look here!" the Red Queen cried. "The dog would lose its temper, wouldn't it?"

"Perhaps it would!" Alice replied cautiously.

"Then if the dog went away, its temper would remain!" the Queen exclaimed.

Alice said, as gravely as she could, "They might go different ways." But she couldn't help thinking to herself, "What dreadful nonsense we are talking!"

Nonsense indeed! But very clever nonsense, for it demonstrates that language commonly used in arithmetical situations can make both sense and nonsense at the same time.

A typical example of the confusion of meanings in the mind of a child is shown by the remark of a little girl who, in play, fitted together a very long line of Unifex cubes, set a symbol cap 1 at the end, and then announced triumphantly that she had made "a long one". Every teacher can tell stories of similar confusion in the use of number language, and of errors due to imperfect understanding.

The little boy who turned to his teacher to state a new discovery—that "there's a one and a nought at each end"—clearly had no idea of the significance of the symbols shown above and had fitted the parts of the jig-saw together by manual dexterity alone. His task was quite valueless. Such stories make us smile. They should make us think.

How can we be sure that the children we are teaching have a clear understanding of number language? Only by: (a) arranging for them plenty of number experiences, and (b) talking with them about it. Our only means of access to children's minds is what they say, and what they do. Sum books which contain errors tell a plain story of mis-understanding; yet children are still treated as though the fault were theirs when their sums are wrong. The fault is not theirs: it is ours.

So much is known today of the ways in which children structure number concepts,[1] and of the necessary slow and careful steps which contribute to this process, that teachers should have little difficulty in giving to every child satisfactory and pleasurable arithmetical experience which will grow into firm and unshakeable understanding.

The main difficulties teachers have are:

1. The discarding of prejudices and habits of formal teaching.

2. The provision of a generous supply of suitable materials for learning.

3. Curbing their own impatience to get children working theoretically (on paper).

"Many children of the ages of 5, 6 and 7 years can and do acquire a kind' of parrot notion of ordination and cardination, and the ability to carry out simple arithmetical calculations; but the underlying concepts not being present, lack of understanding, confusion and discouragement frequently result later."[2]

Teachers are very anxious that their pupils shall *calculate abstractly*. The ability to handle numbers in a conventional way, to produce cor-

---

[1] N. Isaacs: *The Growth of Understanding in the Young Child.*
    New Light on Children's Ideas of Number.
[2] E. Churchill: *Counting and Measuring in the Infants' School.*

rect answers to mechanically worked addition, subtraction, multiplication and division sums has traditionally been regarded as showing mastery over arithmetical ideas. We know that nothing is further from the truth, and that ability to perform mechanical operations of this kind can and often does mask many gaps in true number understanding which show up when a memory lapse occurs or when the calculations have a different twist. The cracks have merely been papered over.

It is for the Infants' teacher to ensure the walls rise without cracks; in order to do this she must abandon the idea of traditional 'sums' in the Infants' school and think in terms of children talking and doing things with numbers. Only when much of this has been accomplished should she think in terms of writing. "Sums," said a wise educationalist of today, "should be a record of things *done*."[1]

An essential first step is the *acquisition of number language*. Churchill says, "The little child hears the language of number, and picks up many of the words. This does not mean that he endows them with a mathematical meaning, and he must be allowed time to feel his way into the language as did his forebears."

There was a time when Infants' teachers tried to insist a child restrict his number thinking about the word 'five' to:

The fact is that 'five' to an infant really means something like the diagram opposite, which is 'five' in the real-life situation. And out of this medley of ideas a child has to grasp a concept of 'five' which he can manipulate at will, and apply to any mathematical or practical situation. This stage is a long way off for the Infant and can only grow slowly through much practical experience.

An outline follows of the kind of number experience which the Family-grouped classroom makes available. As with reading and writing it must provide experience at all levels so that children may advance as slowly or as rapidly as suits each individual, and regress at any stage of learning to a point at which they feel secure.

Preliminary Stages

Much number talk will arise from natural situations (e.g. counting and registration). A useful device associated with registration is a coloured clothes peg for every child (red for boys and blue for girls). As each child comes into the classroom he clips his peg to a wire stretched along the wall or the teacher's table. Later in the day the pegs may be counted and the information translated onto a chart.

---

[1] L. C. Schiller, formerly H.M. Staff Inspector for Primary Schools.

106

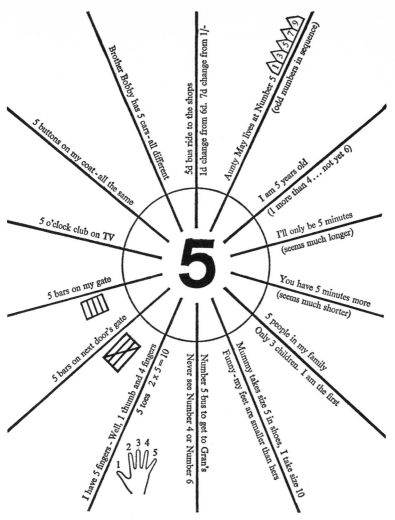

Some aspects of 'five' in real life situation

Further information can be extracted from this by older children such as, "On which day of the week did most (or fewest) children attend?"

There will be things to handle (pegboards, towers, rings, blocks, shapes, etc.); things to sort, match and count; simple games of the 'track' or 'fill the square' variety which are played with dice and counters. A teacher recommends one shelf of games for *any* child to play, and another shelf of more difficult games for the use of children at a more advanced stage.

The use of numbers in many classroom situations should not be forgotten. Pages of scrapbooks should be numbered, and boxes containing play apparatus should have the number of articles contained written on the lid. Counting and checking will have a double purpose.

Talking with individual children and younger groups about such situations is an essential part of the classroom work. The teacher should always be on the look-out for opportunities to refer to meaningful number situations.

Next Stage of Number Learning

When the children begin to use number language with understanding, and can count (make a one-to-one correspondence) the teacher can talk with them about counting with cubes or on the 'counting ladder'—"counting one on; counting two back". Pattern matching with pegs, beads and counters becomes more exact.

Number games become more difficult, and scores are kept with peas or beans, sticks, counters or other tallying devices. Grouping and regrouping is done with beads, conkers, the flannel-graph or pegboards. The understanding of relationships and patterns within a group is essential to the appreciation of conservation[1] without which arithmetical calculation must be unsure. Early play with Cuisenaire, Dienes or other structured apparatus can begin. Drawing can also be linked: "Draw five cars in a row." "Now in a bunch."

Money will become familiar in the play situation of 'going shopping' and one teacher says all her first 'sums' are related to money as this is a familiar medium of calculation for so many children.

Measuring play with foot rules, yard sticks, tape measures and so on brings understanding of the language of measurement and of such terms as tall, short, little, high and long. Similarly, a meaningful vocabulary of weight will arise from balancing and counting with stones, acorns, beans and bricks. Light, heavy, more than and less than will really have significance. Waterplay leads to measuring water in terms of cups, bottles, jugs and jars; the vocabulary of capacity should be slowly fed in, but at first: "Three spoonsful of water fill the doll's cup," rather than, "Two pints make one quart."

The teacher draws attention to shapes and sizes. Examples of scrap books children like to make, which in turn increase observation and organize knowledge are: "A Book about Space; Round Things; Straight Lines."[2]

Ideas about fractions are easily understood in the practical world:

---

[1] N. Isaacs: *New Light on Children's Ideas of Number*.
[2] For many helpful suggestions for stimulating materials and interesting books—
G. Allen and others: *Scientific Interests in the Primary School*.

"half a stick of plasticine, a quarter of tea, a halfpenny, half an hour."

Writing and drawing are useful with all these basic number ideas. The essential things are (a) to record what is done, and (b) to see that experiences are rich and plentiful.

Before number ideas can be accurately used, they must be secure—ordination, cardination, seriation, conservation and reversibility must be firmly established. They cannot be taught—they can only be acquired by well organized, unhurried experience. Some children take longer than others, but all can do it. "It should not be thought the growth of the ability to see structure is the prerogative of the able child."[1]

Further Stages

For those who are ready, the following should be included: counting in groups forward and backward on the 'counting ladder' or with counters and sticks (multiplication and division); counting to 100 on a long counting ladder; making 'sums' upon it and recording them. Children brought up in this way will make their own sums and do better than if they take them from books. Sometimes, however, they will enjoy using books for stimulation and practice in an acquired skill.

Further stages also include the introduction of the abacus for place value; building up of 'tables' by grouping (but for practice use table cards or multiplication card apparatus rather than insist on rote-learning); more difficult number games; estimating (the good guess) followed by weighing and measuring; comparison of weights of parcels, heights of people, lengths and widths of rooms; charts and histograms on squared paper (children will realize that this is another way of recording information from which further information can be extracted).

Practical Routines

The following conversation took place in a classroom during the summer:

6-year-old: "Isn't it hot! (Suddenly) We haven't taken the temperature lately."

Teacher: "Would you like to do it now?"

6-year-old: "Can Colin come with me?"

After this, temperatures were taken daily. The teacher said, "It was the children's idea—I didn't have to remind them."

---

[1] L. Sealey and V. Gibbon: *Communication and Learning in the Infants' School.*
E. Churchill: *Counting and Measuring in the Infants' School*

Many records can be kept as a matter of course—names added to "Books of the Months" as children have birthdays; daily attendance; children who can tie shoe-laces; heights of growing plants; weights of growing pets; birds feeding at the bird table, and so on. In such situations estimating should be encouraged: "How many do you think?"

Number Through Play and Other Interests

Almost every play or interest includes a number element. The prehistoric animal interest (page 92) and the school model project (page 95) were both instructive arithmetically. Simpson and Alderson describe how number came into a play situation when children made an "Air Force Canteen".[1] Water was measured for 'beer' and money was used for fares in a train (constructed of wooden boxes) for the journey to the canteen. They also describe how a drama performance of 'The Frog Prince' led to the making of posters and handbills, the numbering of seats and selling of tickets and programmes.

Here is a 7-year-old writing of something *done*:

"We made some water clocks. When we made them we got some water from the tap and filled our tins up to a crayon mark. Before I filled it up I punched two holes in my tin. Keith punched one hole in his tin. Keith's tin took 5 minutes to empty because I punched 2 holes in my tin it took 3 minutes to empty."

These are natural situations, stimulated by the children's own interests, accepted as part of life, and not as 'sums'. More than 30 years ago Susan Isaacs pointed the way: "We kept the children's . . . understanding of number and arithmetical processes constantly related to their practical interests."[2]

Number is not just for the number lesson; it is there all the time for the children to use and the teacher to bring to their notice at any moment of any day.

Since the first publication of this book the Nuffield Mathematics Teaching Project has been launched. Its publications offer much practical help to the Infants' teacher.

Summary

This chapter has dealt with intellectual growth—with developing in each child his potential ability to think. We have noted that young children 'think' best in dealing with a practical situation and that stimulus to their thought is *doing*, in interaction with materials and situations, with books, with each other and the teacher. If this positive experience is denied them, the development of the power to think abstractly is made more difficult. Children should leave the

---

[1] D. Simpson and D. Alderson: *Creative Play in the Infants' School.*
[2] S. Isaacs: *Intellectual Growth in Young Children.*

Infants' school wanting to seek information for themselves, and with some ability to order their own learning and organize such facts as they can discover. However, none of these processes can be carried very far, because the children are young, and in some children they will hardly seem to exist, except perhaps in attitude.

Infants' teachers realize that an atmosphere conducive to the growth of such an attitude is most easily cultivated when anxiety, both for pupil and teacher, is at a minimum. The authors have already given their reasons why anxiety is at a minimum in the stability of a Family-grouped class. Where the teacher has time to know her children as people, she sees with great satisfaction the abilities of all beginning to blossom as they grow towards their seventh and eighth years.

Wall, writing of the many primary schools which "even yet, concentrate almost exclusively upon the attainment of mechanical perfection in the basic skills", says: "It seems both educationally and psychologically sounder to view the intellectual aspects of the early years of primary education as aiming to equip a child with certain modes or techniques of thinking and expression. For later learning, as well as for adult living, he needs a mastery of verbal thinking and verbal communication; he needs . . . the beginnings of a command of numerical thinking, ordering, enumeration, comparison of spaces, volumes and sequences; . . . and enlightened curiosity and insight into the objective evaluation of observed facts which is the basis of empirical science and scientific thinking . . ."[1]

To launch all this satisfactorily at the Infants' level is a heavy responsibility, and one difficult to discharge. But, recognizing that failure is cumulative, we realize how essential it is that we shall not fail the children we teach.

Talk of intellectual development often includes reference to the 'stretching' of the able child—regardless of the fact that 'stretch', when carried far enough, ends in "break". Teachers find that the methods discussed in this chapter extend not only the capabilities of the able child, but also of all children. Undoubtedly, many school children are under-functioning, even at Infants' school level.

Looking again at the equation at the head of this chapter: *Maturation* × *Experience* = *Achievement*, we must consider afresh the experiences we offer as *our* contribution to children's achievements. Says N. Isaacs: "The normal environment of the conventional school is far closer to the negative than the positive end of the scale of procedure for optimum growth."

That was written in 1955. It is still true in 1965. Will it be so in 1975?

---

[1] W. Wall: *Education and Mental Health.*

6

Class Lessons

One of the tasks of education is to place before the developing mind a succession of imaginative works, each of which is beyond the present range of emotions, but not beyond the range of sympathy.[1]

Many teachers feel that they can work effectively with individuals or groups in the teaching of reading, writing and number yet they wonder to what extent class teaching should be retained for story-times, poetry, music, physical and religious education when classes are of mixed ages.

The problem seems to fall into two parts: (a) is it possible or desirable to take such lessons with less than the whole class, and (b) if all the class is included, can the subject matter be suitable both for the rising 5-year-old, beginning his Infants' school life, and for the 7-year-old who is nearing the end of his?

Each of the lessons referred to will be dealt with in turn in this chapter, but with brevity. A book written about each would be necessary to do them justice; the authors are mainly concerned to show how teachers do, in practice, deal with the problems in (a) and (b), and briefly to consider their reasons.

Religious Education

The problems associated with the religious teaching of Infants are not primarily those of variations in the ages of a class. They are basically a matter of personal conviction and commitment, and of an appreciation of the dangers of teaching 'too much—too young'. Children of Infant-years (i.e. 4-plus to 7-plus) are in the broad phase of development in which they are differentiating between fantasy and reality; between the objective and subjective world. Between these two worlds there is a considerable overlap, and the child-mind fluctuates in its ability to distinguish between them. Mental and emotional life is egocentric—centred on the self, its intimate experiences and immediate relationships. Even at 7-plus years the ability to think realistically and feel altruistically is only partially developed. Teachers are increasingly aware of misinterpretation by children of their early religious teaching.[2] This is not necessarily to suggest they should receive none.

---

[1] D. Griffiths: *The Psychology of Literary Appreciation.*
[2] D. Ainsworth: *An Aspect of the Growth of Religious Understanding of Children Aged 5–11 years* (Unpublished Dip. Ed. dissertation Univ. Manchester 1961).

"The child's spiritual development and education towards spiritual maturity is of greater importance than ever before in the history of our civilization."[1]

There is a growing feeling that general attitudes over the whole area of school life exercise as great an influence on spiritual development as the religious education lesson. "The influence of the teacher of Infants is pervasive throughout the day in a total approach to knowledge and encompasses the whole of the school experience of the child."[2] Teachers and religious education advisory committees are trying to reassess the spiritual experiences the small child receives in school lessons based on Bible teaching, or in times of communal worship. It is being more generally realized that some of the teaching, far from enriching children's spiritual life, has confused religious ideas with those of myth and magic, and given to some a superficial religious vocabulary unrelated to their own experience, imperfectly understood and very liable to misinterpretation.

The area of this vitally important subject is so vast, and the range of ideas which would be opened by an adequate discussion so wide, that having superficially stated the problem, the authors will do little more than describe ways in which teachers and headteachers deal with the organization of religious education in the Family-grouped class.

1. There are some schools where religious education takes place entirely within the classroom. It is felt that the personal influence of the teacher and the relationships of the children with her and with one another are the growing point for cultivation of love and reverence for God.

In these schools worship, prayer and simple instruction are linked with an interest in nature, interrelationships of the children as shown in kindness and thoughtfulness, and with parents, brothers and sisters. For talk about a Creator of wonderful and beautiful things, a God who cares for all, and of the goodness and strength of Jesus, natural occasions are sought such as birthdays, Christmas, seasonal changes, news items brought by the children themselves of perhaps personal experience of illness or sorrow, or of disasters of various kinds.

An act of worship with the whole school, except on rare and special occasions, is felt to be too overwhelming and meaningless an experience; daily worship takes place in the classroom. Speaking of her experience in watching such a class, a student teacher (herself antagonistic towards religious education in schools) said, "I was moved, as I have never been moved before, by school worship. The children stood up to say their prayers as naturally as they performed every other act in the class setting. A child said the prayer and they were all with

---

[1] R. Goldman: *Studies in Education: First Years in School.*
[2] ibid.

her; nobody peeped through their fingers or touched another child. The act of worship was brief, but it was profound; they were a real family. Then they all set to work."

2. Most schools have a daily period of simple communal worship which may include music, something of natural beauty to look at (flowers, leaves or shells, etc.), or language related to the experience of the children yet which is designed to evoke a sense of reverence. An attitude of quiet serenity and content on the part of children and teacher is sought, unmarred by reproof or irritation.

If these are the ingredients, and the time is short, it is felt that such worship will be associated with peace, security and pleasure even for the youngest. The children often sit in natural groups with their teacher in 'arena' fashion, so that they may see each other and share one another's feeling.

There are many indications that children value class and school worship and that it gives experience in depth which nothing else can give. It is missed by them when they do not have it. Instances have been given of children saying, "We haven't been in the hall today," or, "Aren't we going to say our prayers?"

Some Junior and Infants' schools describe periods when the Infants join in worship with the Juniors. Such occasions are especially valuable when the older children conduct the act of worship, or when they make contributions of recorder or orchestral music, or of prayers, readings or drama. Such participation is seen by the younger children to be meaningful to the older ones, and this gives it an impact and value greater than that evoked by any adult.

However, "joining Infants and Juniors together for worship is perhaps useful as a weekly event, where a whole school community may meet together, but as a daily occurrence it is not to be commended."[1]

3. Sometimes older Infants are withdrawn from their classes for a shared religious experience together with the headteacher. It might consist of direct religious teaching (based on one of the agreed syllabuses); talks or stories relating to ethical standards which young children try to establish (helping others, resisting selfishness, resisting the temptation to steal or lie); further experience of music, poetry, pictures, natural or man-made objects of wonder or mystery; and sometimes a special contribution to the daily service is prepared.

Although the general principle of retaining the Family Group is not to be lightly set aside, some headteachers feel that these special times with her help the older children by giving a special significance to the subject, a tacit recognition of the importance of the ideas pursued, and an awareness of their own greater maturity and responsibility. The

---

[1] R. Goldman: *First Years in School: Children's Spiritual Development.*

class teacher also has valuable moments to devote herself to the younger children alone.

Discussion with teachers and heads about religious education has made it clear that schools are taking a fresh look at accepted practices. They are feeling the need to present children with simple, meaningful spiritual experience, to carry religious attitudes through the whole day rather than confine them to the religious education 'story lesson', and are quietly finding individual ways of doing this.

Literature: Stories and Poetry

Critics of Family Grouping, who describe as 'impossible' the task of selecting stories which will appeal to children of 5 and 7 years, forget the family circle of a bygone era, when mother or father sat reading to a group of children of various ages, perhaps on a Sunday afternoon, with the youngest lying on a hearthrug near the fire. Such romantic times have their modern counterpart in the family group of various ages around the television set.

It is true that in school we hope, by understanding each child, to place before them material particularly suited to their individual intellectual or emotional needs. Often we can only guess at what those needs may be.

In practice, teachers try to meet them in many ways, perhaps telling or reading a story or poem to a small group of children at a time, leaving the children free to decide whether they will come to listen or not. Two provisos are usually made: those who do not come must be quietly occupied and those who join in must remain quietly seated with the group until the end. By these means the teacher gives herself the maximum chance to 'evoke the magic'.[1]

Teachers often select stories for different levels of maturation and tell them to all the class. Children of 4 to 6 years are usually interested in 'family' stories and those with play interest; stories which are cumulative or include repetition; jingles or nonsense stories in which they can join; and in animal stories, which often, by identification of self with the animal, provide an outlet for fears and anxieties.

It is interesting to note that when a choice is given, the older children often ask for such 'childish' stories, or come voluntarily to hear them many times over. There is clearly some satisfaction or sense of security for them in the rehearing. Says Vicars Bell: "Fears and anxieties are as deep-rooted as eye teeth—they won't come out at one pull. It is for this reason that the child never seems to tire of hearing these tales over and over again."[2] Adults too read and reread literature which not only satisfies or pleases them deeply, but which yields greater depth of meaning when reread.

---

[1] V. Bell: *On Learning the English Tongue.*
[2] ibid.

Stories selected for older Infants will usually be longer, perhaps of the serial or 'group' type, and they will contain more difficult language and range further afield in imagination. They often include folk and fairy stories, stories involving people and places of far away or long ago, myths, legends and tales of heroes.[1] Here again the choice is sometimes left to the younger children to listen or be quietly occupied.

Hollamby says: "When a child may choose whether or not he will join a story group, a number will quietly listen after the story has begun. Some will continue their own occupations as well as listen, but others will creep nearer to the group and give their undivided attention to the story. It is right for a child to feel this situation is permissible, for sometimes he is the only one who can decide whether the job in hand or the story is best for him."[2]

Absolute understanding of every word is unnecessary. Meaning is often sensed and absorbed by the context and flow of the story. Meaning should not be hammered home, or questions asked—except by the children of the teacher. Hume[3] suggests children enjoy stories according to their mood and there is a good deal of evidence from teachers which confirms this. It is certain that older children sometimes like to regress to stories suited to their earlier years, though the youngest children may find difficulty in understanding or concentrating on the themes and language suitable for older children. However, they do seem to enjoy the quiet pursuit of some pleasant pastime while the older ones are gathered around the teacher attentively listening. It is not always possible for us to know what a child requires but he will take what he needs from what we offer and reject the rest.

A teacher tells of the remark made by one of a small group of Junior children who owing to the illness of a teacher had been amalgamated with the Infants' class for the afternoon. As they left the classroom after hearing the story of "The Red Canoe", which had been intended to interest the 6 to 7-year-olds, one turned to another and said, "I think that's in the library—let's go and get it out."

Stories presented need to be of good quality. A story should be examined for the quality of its content, its aspects of special interest, the language used and the completeness of the theme it contains.

This is no easy task. But it becomes worthwhile if we remember that story-time is "more than a period of amusement". It is a time when a very special atmosphere may be achieved, an atmosphere of repose and eagerness, of response and participation, when, gathered round the

---

[1] Refer to K. Cather: *Educating by Story Telling*.
  M. Shedlock: *The Art of the Story Teller*.
  L. Terman and M. Lims: *Children's Reading*.
[2] L. Hollamby: *Young Children Living and Learning*.
[3] A. Hume: *Learning and Teaching in the Infants' School*.

teacher, the children may go through 'magic casements' and experience depths of shared emotion and a heightened sense of shared pleasure. It is a time treasured by most teachers and looked forward to by all children. One of the worst crimes in the teacher's calendar is for the headteacher or a visitor to intrude and destroy this atmosphere.

Through stories, a child's hunger for further experience and for interpretation of life is partially satisfied. By identification with the people and creatures in the stories he may achieve outlets for unconscious urges, and a measure of catharsis for emotional stress. Interest is aroused in new people and places; he is provided with new food for imagination, that mental digestive process which grows by what it feeds on. Last, but not least, his vocabulary will be increased, providing him with new symbols with which to think and to organize his thoughts.

Some schools feel that some of these aims can be better achieved by withdrawing the oldest children for story-time, either putting them with the headteacher or leaving them with one teacher while another takes the younger ones. There is a possible advantage in this, as one teacher observed: "The children make contact with other members of the staff, getting to know them, and they experience the impact of another personality and viewpoint." In one school a syllabus of stories has been drawn up by the headteacher ranging over a period of two to three years, so that a broad spectrum of literature is presented during the Infants' school life.

Poetry

All that has been said of the telling and reading of stories is equally true of poetry.

Children enjoy poems about people, toys, animals, the seasons, special times and occasions; poems which are short or long, sad, jolly, tender, amusing, gay and lyrical. Their special rhythmic quality, the aptness of their language and their embodiment of intense feeling in brevity makes them most valuable and necessary for children.

The Central Committee of Teachers of English of the East and West Ridings of Yorkshire[1] suggests poetry gains by being presented 'incidentally'—as the moment occurs—and not at any planned time. The class should enjoy a few moments of poetry, rhymes or jingles at irregular times of the day, when suitable moments present themselves. This appears to be fairly common practice and times also tend to be the "quiet time after activity, just before dinner or at home time."

This implies on the part of the teacher a sensitivity to the suitable moment, and a good knowledge of children's poems and poetry anthologies. Here the children help too, for where it is the practice of

---

[1] *Poetry and Children.*

teachers to place books of poems, hymns, jingles and ballads in the book corner, and to use them with groups or with the class until many become familiar, the children will say of an incident, "There's a poem about that in such-and-such a book." And they will run to fetch it.

Taken as part of the daily round, poetry is accepted as natural and gives delight. A child's response is immediate, for he is closer to the primitive self of fantasy life and feeling, of nonsense language and rhythm.

As with stories, children enjoy poetry at different levels at different times. The teacher's difficulty is to keep up with a demand which may include "nature poems and poems of human interest, modern and older poems, narrative and lyrical poems, nonsense poems, poems you can act, poems you can chant, poems you can learn by heart, and poems you puzzle over and say to yourself".[1]

All of this is needed. Says Vicars Bell: "Bulk is important, because without it there is no easy familiarity, no habituation, no unconscious growth of standards."[2] One teacher recommends that an anthology always be kept on the table. "You'll always be turning to it."

Another teacher says, "A 7-year-old will often read to the others in spare moments, or in a moment of temporary crisis when the teacher's attention is needed elsewhere." Such reading is sometimes half memorization; the other children may join in, and a small collection of verses and jingles is committed painlessly to memory over a period of two or three years in the class. So literature has become the "crystallization of many types of experience in durable form."[3]

Drama

Much has already been said of the value and importance of dramatic play (see Chapter 3). This is the form now taken by most drama in the Infants' schools. Free choice, children's time, activity periods and the unprogrammed day, all offer children ample opportunity to select make-believe for themselves.

A dressing-up box should be freely available, the home corner used for domestic play, encouragement given to make 'properties' such as hats, masks, painted Indian tunics, fairy wings, wands and crowns. "I become identified with somebody else, and I become that person, animal or thing; I don't act it, I am it now, in this all-important present time."[4]

Children do this at the drop of a hat. There is no need for an

---

[1] H.M.S.O.: *Language: Some Suggestions.*
[2] V. Bell: *On Learning the English Tongue.*
[3] A. Watts: *The Language and Mental Development of the Child.*
[4] D. Jordan: *Studies in Education: The Arts and Current Tendencies in Education: Movement and Dance.*

organized time for 'acting the story' which the class has heard, with a few chosen children prompted by the teacher, laboriously recapitulating the story to the half-interested, half-envious remainder.

Children do reproduce the stories they have heard, but to be a vivid and purposeful experience this must be at their own choice. Dramatic play is a wonderful release for the inhibited child and for those who are immature, but to act to an audience requires a degree of poise and self-possession which such a child may never achieve. But he can become intensely interested in his own choice of dramatic play.

Says Dr. S. T. Orton: "Sir Richard Paget has offered an interesting thesis that the sign language was the first form of systematic language to be developed and that spoken language was largely an outgrowth therefrom."[1] Symbolic gesture, "that part of the language faculty which deals with the emotional moment", is a form of communication which immature or inhibited children can use with one another, but not with an audience or the teacher. By mime, by brief exchange of very short sentences, by monosyllabic remarks, by sign language, such children act out their interest and emotional needs in small self-chosen groups, as others do in more developed ways. The ceaseless demand for the dressing-up clothes and for time to act shows how deep is the need.

Records of activities of all age-groups are teeming with examples of imaginative and dramatic play—kings and queens, soldiers, spacemen, aeronauts, drivers, policemen, robbers, cowboys and Indians, nurses, doctors and so on. How can the teacher-organized acting of stories such as "The Three Little Pigs" compare with this wealth of self-initiated drama? A child needs only a chance to act what he wants to act, and to use his own language for what he wants to say.

The writer saw a little coloured girl bending with compassion over a self-chosen Mary and simply saying, "It's all right; it's only me." She had interpreted with moving dignity the love and the message of the angel Gabriel, in her own way.

"It is difficult to see how the teacher can enter into this kaleidoscopic world, but she can make opportunities for it, and she can observe it."[2] She can also do much to encourage it.

A teacher in a partially Family-grouped school (see Chapter 8) observed that some children were joining together before school in the morning and at free times to mime, through movement and dance, a story which they had created. It had been sparked off by a piece of climbing apparatus, and eventually fused into a wonderfully imaginative and creative whole idea about space, the moon and planets, with

---

[1] S. Orton: *Reading, Writing and Speech Problems in Children.*

[2] D. Jordan: *Studies in Education: The Arts and Current Tendencies in Education: Movement and Dance.*

moonbeams and the sun, some references to Greek mythology, and concepts of fairy stories with kings and queens, and rescues and escapes of princesses from "the strange creatures".

The teacher made available opportunity for practice in the hall and provided music chosen by the children. They were led by a 7-year-old boy especially gifted in movement; each child's cooperation was freely given, and the quality of their movement steadily improved with their own involvement in the story. Smaller children of 5 and 6 years became drawn in, and the numbers reached between 30 and 40. The headteacher said, "The children developed their own discipline."

The whole theme finally lasted 20 minutes or more and was enacted over and over again by the children, who improved it continuously until it became an integrated work of real beauty in which music, drama, dance and literature were included.

Some examples of their writing follow:

"In our play I am a witch and here I am and I throw my arms up in the air when I am playing my zylophone for the lightning flashes and they have to dance because I cast a spell when I am playing my zylophone and the other people are asleep in space."

"In our play I am a witch and I cast a spell on the people and they all stay still because that is what the spell has done, and it is a very strong spell and I am glad too, and this spell draws everyone into space and they dance here and there and I dance with Jayne now because the red queen that is Josephine is in hospital."

"In our play I am a princess. But I am not a musical princess. Jayne S—— plays the Aeolian harp when the strange creatures come from there home called Pluto and Sheena plays the zylophone for the strange creatures as well. Kim plays for the lightning flashes. The lightning flashes live by the tree. There are eight moonbeams there home is on the boxs but they call it Venus. Nobody plays enything for the Moonbeams because nobody wanted to."

Music

Teachers say that many who had anticipated difficulties in organizing music for the Family-grouped class have found it to be easier in practice than they had expected. This is probably because an adventurous and exploratory attitude towards music is now developing in Primary schools. Two or three decades ago, the teaching of art and craft to children was revolutionized, and, initially through the vitalizing influence of Cizek, Dr. Viola and Marion Richardson, the old formal inhibiting methods were abandoned, and the vigorous creative resources of children released. Attitudes to music are being similarly rethought.

Eunice Bailey[1] describes her failure in a formal percussion band

---

[1] E. Bailey: *Discovering Music with Young Children.*

lesson, and refers to the frustrations of the children and the disappointments of teachers.

Edna Mellor holds similar views: "If we really watch little children learning to play as one of a band, do we not often see anxiety and strain on their faces, and does not the amount of training required suggest to the teacher that something is being attempted that the children are not yet ready for?"[1]

Many teachers are dissatisfied with the formal singing lesson, or the class-organized band lesson, and feel their own technique and knowledge to be inadequate. "Back into the cupboard went the instruments, to wait until we had thought again about the children's needs and abilities, and had considered the creative use of the drums, tambourines and triangles."[2]

Some years ago, nobody would have thought it possible that young children could create music. Even with Juniors, tune-making was confined to the formal 'answering phrase' in response to one given by the teacher. This would be conventional in time, shape and length, and be associated with the teaching of musical grammar (notation and pitch).

A revolutionary change is coming over the musical scene, even as it did in the sphere of painting and handiwork. Teachers now know that "children and creativity go hand in hand. The teacher does not need to teach children to be creative, nor to direct or show them how to be creative. Creativeness is there inside of them."[3] This applies as much to the making of music in its many forms as to any other kind of learning.

Thus the field of possible experience opens out, individual contributions increase, and the need for organized class lessons diminishes.

"If the school work is planned in such a way that a large part of the day is children's time in which they are engaged in purposeful work of their own choice, the teacher will be free to take a group in music with children who are at about the same stage of interest and attainment."

Class Work in Music, Singing and Singing Plus

Is there no class music work in Family-grouped classes? Yes, there is. In the words of one young teacher: "In music, all sing together. If the song is a nursery rhyme, the older ones still like to join in. If the song is more difficult the younger ones like to listen and find enjoyment in doing so. This also encourages the ability to listen."

Another teacher says: "I was so bored with singing when I taught the Reception class. They only seemed to be able to manage nursery rhymes and very simple songs. Now the older ones quickly learn harder songs and the little ones soon join in. The standard has risen

[1] E. Mellor: *Education Through Experience in the Infant's School Years.*
[2] E. Bailey: *Discovering Music with Young Children.*
[3] A. Snyder: *Creating Music with Children.*

all round." And a third writes: "For music and story the sensitive teacher can cater for all levels. Emotional maturity does not necessarily depend on age."

All agree that the older children enjoy singing simple songs and nursery rhymes, especially if they are doing it "for the little ones", but they also like to learn folk tunes, easy classics and more difficult children's songs with humorous or lyrical touches. Many songs with a chorus or repetitive phrase such as "Oh No, John" and "My Bonnie Lies Over the Ocean" are very suitable for Family-grouped classes, as the younger ones can join in the chorus.

No piano is necessary—the older children can sustain a vocal line without help. Though it is better if the teacher is able to sing herself, the non-singer can seek the help of a 7-year-old in guiding and leading the younger ones, or use chime bars or glockenspiel to demonstrate a melody.

The children are quite uninhibited about making their own little songs, especially in an atmosphere where creativity is an accepted part of life. The songs may not have perfectly balanced phrases and perhaps it is not always possible to put a time signature to them, but at this stage it is unimportant. A child's spontaneous song is as unformed and lacking in technique as his painting or his writing, but it will also have a similar freshness and individuality.

Songs may be spontaneous vocal doodling, with nonsense words (bibberlee, bobberlee boo) or words suggested by a story or poem. A teacher's suggestion may be the stimulus, "Sing your names to me," or song-making may be encouraged through the use of techniques such as those suggested by Carl Orff.[1]

Children from the youngest to the oldest can join in such music-making. The whole class or only a small group may be involved.

There are excellent opportunities in the class lesson for the informal use of percussion instruments. The days of telling the children exactly what to do are over. "We'll sing 'Golden Slumbers' and Tommy, would you like to find an instrument that goes with it and play with us?" Tommy uses his discretion and chooses a triangle. "Julia, you join in with something else." One or two more instruments may be added in this way. Or a song enlivened by a percussion introduction. "Play something to show that the soldier is coming, John, then we'll all sing 'Oh, Soldier, Soldier, Won't you Marry Me?' " John will almost certainly choose a drum, and he may select someone else to add a gradual crescendo of taps on the cymbal, finishing with a flourish and a clash. Or the whole class may join in a percussion accompaniment to a song they already know. But the contribution is theirs—they are not merely following someone else's instructions. Memory is sometimes used, and repetition too. "That was an interesting pattern you made, John. Play

---

[1] Carl Orff: *Music for Children.*

it again, and we'll all copy you with our hands. Let's keep it going while we sing."

This is real music-making and children accept it naturally, taking from the class lesson inspiration to use in their own 'choosing time'.

Individual and Group Work—Free-chosen Music-making

Art and handiwork are associated in a teacher's mind with colour, pattern and materials of great variety; with fine or detailed work or with bold splashy stuff in two or three dimensions. There is no end to the possibilities we offer children, and the same abundant variety should be avilable in music also.

Music corners in Infants' rooms are being stocked with a variety of instruments—drums, tambourines, triangles, chime bars, bells, little xylophones and glockenspiels, home-made shakers, metal bars and tubes, and with simple music books, copies of hymn books and collections of nursery and other songs, with flannel-graphs for tune-making and with wide-lined manuscript paper.

How shall all this be used? The children are in no doubt. The children "showed us clearly that they would like both to use musical instruments and to know more about them."[1] Put an instrument into the hands of a child and he will never say, "What shall I do?" He will play. And his pleasure will be immediately apparent in his smile.

Children use the material in the music corner just as freely as any other in the classroom. The use of certain instruments such as the drum may have to be restricted at certain times, but even with such restrictions, which may be necessary for the good of all, children have intense pleasure in playing and experimenting either alone or in groups. In such individual personal experience a future love of music will be rooted. Peter Maxwell Davies, the composer, speaking of his experience with boys at Cirencester Grammar School, said, "Only when making music will many children actually listen to it and learn to appreciate it."

Lavish free experience of this kind can be arranged quite easily by teachers who would be described as 'non-musical' just as the 'non-artistic' teacher arranges opportunities for children to paint. Even a teacher with small musical knowledge is presented with starting and growing points. Beginning with whatever a child can do naturally without prompting a teacher can show ways of extending or enriching the work. "Play that pattern again, David. Can you repeat it twice? Let someone else join in and keep a steady beat with you. Would you like me to write your tune down? Then we shall always remember it."

This is the way into musical notation. The sound comes first, the symbol follows. "What is it," asks Vaughan Williams, "which the

---

[1] E. Bailey: *Discovering Music with Young Children.*

composer invents? Not the little black dots which he puts on paper, but the actual sounds those black dots represent . . . The writing of notes is merely a convenience, necessary owing to the comparative feebleness of our memories . . . To hold up this mere convenience as an ideal to be aimed at is surely to put the cart before the horse."[1]

So, for children, the use of notes on flannel-graph or paper takes its proper place, which is to capture and communicate some of the wealth of sound, as written words do for language. But the notes are of small importance compared with the sound.

As children seem naturally to form themselves into groups to play together (making a band) there are many opportunities for the teacher to join with them and to further their efforts.

A teacher says, "Children are able to gain considerable experience through opportunities for creative music-making throughout the day. There is much experiment with sound by the youngest children, and this gradually leads on to the recorder work with the older ones. The children form their own 'band' with recorders and percussion; the younger children play the latter instruments. They sing songs composed by themselves, which are sometimes taught to the whole class. An occasional singing lesson is an advantage."[2]

Music and Other Activities

Where music is accepted as a natural part of the classroom environment it is used wherever it can add life and sparkle to other work. Teachers describe children using instruments to highlight special moments in dramatic play (the tick of the clock, the sound of horses' hoofs, clash of cymbals in a fight, tinkling music for fairies or birds) and they describe children using instruments as a natural means of expression for emotion. Surprising examples have been given.

Three boys came to their teacher one day with a wooden xylophone, a triangle and a pair of cymbals, which were being played by placing them flat together and gently rotating them. They said, "Will you hear our thing? It's called 'The Oodly Door'." The children played a rather mysterious, chilling little piece, with soft tinkling sounds against the rubbing of the cymbals, and a hesitant, meandering tune on the wooden xylophone. They explained, "We was in the library and the door kept coming open, so we made 'The Oodly Door'."

To illustrate the unexpected way in which such creative work may be triggered off, one more example follows:

The same three boys, who often played together, came to play a

---

[1] Vaughan Williams, from the essay 'The Letter and the Spirit' in the collection, *Beethoven's Choral Symphony*.

[2] The class teacher organizing this musical experience for her class is not herself a skilled musician. She does not play the piano and cannot sing, though she has taught herself the recorder. But she has a permissive and helpful attitude towards children's aesthetic work in general.

piece which they called 'Ot Rice'. It consisted of a series of rising and falling passages on the chime bars, interspersed with the chatter of a castanet and a shake or two from the tambourine. To the mystified teacher the children explained, "The rice at dinner time was 'ot, so we made ' 'Ot Rice'."

How can a teacher's suggestions hope to compete with the fertility of such imagination? (They were by no means good little boys either!)

Teachers also describe children suggesting appropriate instruments to illustrate stories told by the teacher. The chime bars strike 12 in Cinderella; each pig has his own special music made with rhythm sticks, triangle or drum tap in The Three Little Pigs; The Three Bears each have a home-made shaker, made from a different-sized tin containing peas, beans or sand.

Children seem to have instinctive, inventive feelings for suitable instruments once they have soaked themselves in musical experience.

Instruments are used for dance and movement. This is a natural development from music and movement lessons, and is greatly enjoyed by children who will make small groups to be Indians, Spanish dancers, fairies and witches, or will just move vigorously and cheerfully about, each dancing or playing in an entirely personal way.

The factor of wide age-ranges seems almost immaterial in a movement lesson. An onlooker writes: "I saw one extremely good music and movement lesson taken with a mixed age-group. It was interesting to see the increased maturity of the movement by older children compared with the younger ones, but it was also interesting to note that in a few instances the younger children outshone the older ones."

A headteacher comments: "Although the control of the older ones becomes finer, they do not interfere with the younger children and vice versa."

Eunice Bailey asserts: "I am sure there is great value in unorganized spontaneous dancing . . . It usually has its roots in some current interest of the children which supplies the essential inspiration."[1]

It is sometimes thought that older children develop better musically if lessons are given to them separately and this is organized according to the talents of the staff. Sometimes the headteacher takes the 7-year-olds from two or three classes together for singing or for music and movement, or a gifted teacher interchanges with a non-musician. But it is fairly common practice, even so, for group and individual work, based on the music corner in the classroom or hall, to be part of the regular, free-chosen experience of the children at all ages.

Musical Growth

All this is vital musical food. What other nutrition should be given?

---

[1] E. Bailey: *Discovering Music with Young Children.*

However musically inexperienced a teacher may be, there are resources in gramophones and radios available to all.

A child who has made 'dancing music' of his own will be all the more interested to listen to the 'Chinese Dance' or 'The Dance of the Sugar-Plum Fairy' from Tchaikovsky's 'Nutcracker Suite'. The child who likes to play a percussion instrument will be very receptive to the excitement of Rimsky Korsakov's 'Capriccio Espagnole'. Listening sessions should be short and varied. Children will then ask again and again for favourites and welcome hearing something new.

Talents of available adults should always be exploited. Teachers, visitors and parents often have hidden skills, and can be persuaded to play their particular instrument or to sing to the children. Older children in a Junior or Secondary school are often delighted at the chance to play or sing to an audience, and such concerts are always very successful, especially in the intimate atmosphere of the classroom, as children are particularly susceptible to performances by other children.

Some 7-year-olds were invited by their Junior school to a concert by professional instrumentalists. The experience delighted them and stimulated their own music-making. In "Our Book of Percussion Instruments" they drew and wrote about the kettledrum, a rattle, side-drum, tambourine, tom-tom, gong, piano, bass-drum and bells, and included such captions as: "This is the side-drum. It is usually played on a stand and it has a sound like horses galloping."

Other listening experiences include guessing games with musical instruments, naming, pointing with closed eyes and 'hearing' from the quietest sound to the loudest, and the 'Music and Movement', 'Time and Tune', or 'Music Box' broadcasts of the B.B.C.

Several teachers allow groups of children to follow the B.B.C. programme by themselves while they remain with the rest of the class. As the children choose to do this and are usually those who particularly enjoy music, they can be relied upon to work well.

To the teacher who has thought of music as a once-a-week class lesson in the hall, activities such as these may seem a waste of time which may better be spent in practice of the intellectual skills. Sir Herbert Read calls for a shift of emphasis towards cultural and aesthetic education, reminding us that the "general purpose of education is to foster what is individual in each human being."[1]

Those who make time to foster musical creativity in little children describe how their enjoyment and satisfaction light up the whole personality, and general progress as well as knowledge of music is quickened. Musically deprived children are impoverished in personality; they have one less means of expression, and one less source

---

[1] H. Read: *Education Through Art.*

of satisfaction. They are denied the use of a unique language which they can use instinctively and with acute insight.

Family Grouping does not seem to place any obstacle, rather the contrary, in the way of children using this language effectively, or of increasing their knowledge of it.

Physical Education

"Individuals differ greatly in mental and physical attributes, and so each will use the movement factors in different but equally effective ways."[1]

The modern approach to Physical Education follows changes in other spheres of learning. Beginning with the capabilities of each individual it moves on to encourage full personal development of them.

The various types of lesson—gymnastics, indoor and outdoor games—each when analysed can be seen to rest upon the personal improvement and development of each child. The development may be in management and control of the body, in the growth of a specific skill such as skipping or ball-throwing, in cooperation with others, or in manipulating the body on a climbing frame. But it remains personal and individual to each child. No longer are children required to conform to orders. The teacher's task is far more subtle—she has to encourage and stimulate each child to put effort into his task, to increase his own challenge to himself in complexity or duration of concentration, and yet not develop a competitive atmosphere, with one child trying to beat another; or an imitative one in which the children copy each other or the teacher.

This is a task of great difficulty, yet it does not appear that the age-range of 5 to 7 years makes it more difficult except where space is limited, when there may be danger of younger children being knocked down. They are not so steady on their feet or as nimble in changing direction or in steering a path between each other.

A case can here be made for joining groups of 7-year-olds together for vigorous exercise which might otherwise be restricted. Otherwise some kinds of organized grouping may be helpful—the youngest children on the floor, the older ones on the climbing frame, the middle group using stools and mats and then a change around.

But as this kind of grouping is a recognized feature of the physical education lesson Family Grouping is not disadvantageous. An onlooker describes such a class working on Essex apparatus. The children had, as it happened, been given complete freedom of choice. "As there was plenty of space, there was no overcrowding on any particular piece of the apparatus, and the children were using it at their own level. The 5-year-olds were not in any way worried by the older children. They were all quite happy trying out the possibilities of the apparatus

[1] *Educational Gymnastics* (London County Council publication, number 4162).

and gaining confidence. The older ones were using the apparatus well and were putting in a considerable amount of effort."

It has been suggested that the younger children may perhaps try to imitate older ones in daring feats on the climbing apparatus, and that this may be a source of danger. It must of course be guarded against, and discouraged if it should occur. Other teachers, however, give it as their experience that unless actively stimulated to try more difficult feats, the younger children seem content to discover by gradual means the challenges of the apparatus, and do not venture beyond their personal limit of safety. This varies greatly from the child who refuses to do anything but sit and watch, to the confident climber who grips competently with hands and feet and moves with agile assurance over the whole range of the apparatus.

Critics comment on the older child who may be under-exerting himself. As there will be a dozen or so children of comparable age in the class against whose prowess he can, if he wishes, match his own, it seems unlikely that the presence of younger children will discourage effort. There is more likely to be some other inhibiting factor, such as poor health, fatigue, unsuitable clothing, shyness, fear or simply that his imagination has not been captured; he may be merely uninterested.

The tasks which the teacher sets to older children will be in general more complex. They will require more bodily skill, more sustained effort and possibly involve some memorization (the beginning of making a 'movement phrase'). However, since all will respond at their own level of capacity and these levels will differ much even in children of the same age, it would seem that teachers who claim it is quite possible to deal adequately with movement, games and apparatus work with the Family-grouped class are right.

To conclude the following quotation from a report made by a young teacher of a Family-grouped class is given:

"I did not use any special method at all in grouping the children but asked them to stand by their chosen piece of apparatus. I found that the new entrants chose that which they felt confident on, often liking to jump from the stools. According to their degree of confidence the older children chose the more advanced apparatus. By observing, the younger children progressed rapidly to the Southampton-Cave apparatus, and only the more timid children did not go near it. There were some older children who would not venture on it.

"Seeing the older children on the Cave and the scrambling net seemed to give the younger ones confidence. They were able to progress at their own pace and just by experience they were able to see the range of movement which could be done, and sometimes they would work at the level of the older children.

"There was no interference between ages, and all felt they were

Another self-organized music-making group of 5, 6 and 7 years

Family-grouped classes using apparatus (see page 127)

attempting the possible—not the impossible. Some of the activities were very skilled and performed at what seemed to me to be dizzy heights, but I did not stop them as I felt they knew their own capabilities. To restrict them would introduce an element of fear and sap confidence."

7

The Teacher

If we analyse the psychology of enlightened teacher-pupil relationships we find three common components: 1. consideration, 2. a sense of humour and 3. a philosophy of growth.[1]

Role of the Infants' Teacher

The role of the Infants' teacher has undergone considerable change in recent years.

Most adults recall the teacher of their childhood as a kindly domineering person whom they may have respected, liked and even loved, but with whom their relationship centred around the word obedience. Teachers told children what to do, supplied information and arranged tasks which were performed without option. Good behaviour was in performing the task as rapidly and competently as possible, then waiting docilely until told what to do next. To show initiative was seldom a virtue and independence was not encouraged. A teacher centred her efforts upon keeping the class, which was nearly always very large, orderly and fully employed, with the children working as nearly as possible at the same level. Conformity to a set level of attainment was required—keeping together in reading (to peep at the page ahead was an offence), and working a set number of sums correctly. Much of lesson preparation consisted of marking children's work for correction, or improving it in some way, neatening edges of handwork, taking out poor knitting and restarting it, and pulling out bad stitches in needlework. The end-product was often demonstrated in advance, and was to be copied or imitated as accurately as possible; work badly done might be returned several times.

The teacher worked hard. Maintaining order was sometimes difficult, partly because of the pressure needed to keep children busy on tasks which they might not be enjoying. Relaxation was found in periods of crayoning or manipulating plasticine, and such work was normally judged by the criterion of how closely it resembled an identifiable object. Play was discouraged, and the teacher was the accepted fountain of inspiration and effort.

Her role is now profoundly different. So different that sometimes teachers feel themselves insecurely balanced between the two dangers of over-directing children and of opting out of class management altogether.

---

[1] A. Gesell and F. Ilg: *The Child from Five to Ten.*

The teacher of today 'teaches' in several ways; by providing appropriate material and conditions for using it; by working and playing with children; and by direct teaching. Her function is to provide an environment for development, and part of that environment is herself.[1] The teacher is the centre of the classroom situation and its life now revolves *around* her rather than radiates *from* her.

It is the teacher who (a) ensures provision of materials and apparatus. (Some of this will be standard provision from Local Authorities or educational suppliers, selected for its particular relevance to stages of development; some will be made by the teacher and some will be brought in by the children); (b) organizes the classroom along workshop lines and plans its arrangement. With the help of the children she maintains its order and introduces aesthetic touches; (c) arranges learning situations and opportunities for purposeful play; (d) assists children's growth by teaching and guiding; (e) promotes an atmosphere of happiness, self-help, mutual respect and cooperation; and (f) establishes standards.

In all this she makes use of children's drive and initiative, their sociability and their involvement in their own learning.

This way of teaching has novel aspects when compared with more traditional procedures; it postulates a technique which can only be acquired by actually doing it. Some teachers describe feeling their way towards it through a gradual adaptation of traditional methods to a lesser degree of formality. Some schools, as a considered policy, make a radical overall change (see Chapter 9). Schools which have adapted their methods either slowly or suddenly all refer to teachers' developing capacities to use their new freedom. "I see opportunities that I never saw before," or "I can't imagine teaching in any other way now," or "The longer you do it the easier it becomes," are the kind of comments frequently made.

As a teacher's capacity for using opportunities increases and as the children become more competent to help themselves,[2] pressures lessen. As a teacher becomes more relaxed she is better able to watch the interplay of personalities in the class, to see below the surface to underlying motivation and to bring a fresh vision to bear on difficulties encountered by individuals in intellectual and emotional situations.

Days develop a more leisurely tempo. "There is something seriously wrong with a school," said Dr. Hughes in 1937, "in which life is a mad race against time."[3]

---

[1] "Education is never an operation performed by A on B but always a cooperation between living wholes." M. Jacks: *Total Education.*

[2] Speaking of the first day of each new term, a teacher says, "I get out some of the larger equipment; the older children help me and by 11 o'clock it's just as if there'd never been a break." How many teachers in conventional classrooms can say this?

[3] A. Hughes and E. Hughes: *Learning and Teaching.*

Working *with* the children rather than directing them *to* work gives a teacher the opportunity to know her own equipment and how it may best be used or supplemented. She finds frequent occasions for useful notes, perhaps of some aspect of a child's progress or need, or a starting point for new work, or ways of developing work already begun.

The interpretation of 'activity methods' in which the children are active and the teacher passive is as undesirable as the authoritarian concept of the active teacher and the passive children. Both should make contributions to the teaching-learning situation which only each can; a continuous "interaction between person and person".[1] This greatly enriches classroom life, exploiting as it does the continuous flow of children's ever-changing interests.

But freedom and initiative on the children's part imply patience, consideration and encouragement on the teacher's, and a considerable degree of ability to adapt plans which must be broadly made in advance.

Child-Teacher Relationships

Because of the length of time in which teacher and children work together, relationships can grow slowly. Rapport cannot be achieved in days, or even weeks. In due course the child knows the teacher's ways, and then has long continuity of teaching methods. The teacher gradually learns her pupils' characters and capacities, begins to discover how best to cultivate them, and recognizes as temporary the plateaux when learning seems to pause and slow up. She can also tolerate ambivalent behaviour which may stem from conflicts between a growing need for independence and the continuing requirement of security and protection. When fully established, such rapport produces a most satisfactory resilience in pupil-teacher relationships and the child feels secure, the teacher confident, in the mutual understanding and respect which are the core of it. If children move too quickly or too often this rapport is lost; perhaps even worse, the ability of both child and teacher to establish it anew with fresh individuals may ultimately be damaged through repeatedly having to start again.

Parent-Teacher Relationships

The rapport between teacher and child develops over a period to include mutual trust and understanding with his parents, or at least with his mother. More than one psychologist has referred to the tension experienced by a child, "with his double bonds".[2] Again, this personal relationship cannot grow overnight. When teacher and

---

[1] L. Reid: *Philosophy and Education.*
[2] A. Gesell and F. Ilg: *The Child from Five to Ten.*

parents know one another long enough it can be cultivated quite naturally. But if it is not there, nothing can replace it. "There seems to be a therapeutic value in a child's seeing his teacher and parent talking amicably."[1] The child realizes all is right with his two worlds.

The 'Problem' of discipline

Many teachers speak of the way in which Family Grouping resolves disciplinary difficulties. This is almost certainly because of the deep satisfaction which the children find in school. Of course, Family-grouped classes have no monopoly of such satisfactions.

Discontent often provokes misconduct, having sprung from a lack of satisfying work. If occupations are too easy a child is bored: if they are too difficult he is frustrated or depressed. Where work is individually chosen or matched to his need and ability, boredom and frustration do not occur. This, together with verbal freedom, and creative work and play with its fantasy-release, reduces the incidence of rebellious or defiant conduct to negligible proportions. Teachers say, "I hardly ever even have to grumble," and "There's never any disciplinary difficulty." In one eloquent phrase spoken by the head-teacher of a large city school where social and emotional problems abound, "The difficult ones become undifficult."

In the most natural possible way 'discipline' is translated into 'self-discipline' and when times of ill-temper or aggression do occur, suggestion,[2] persuasion or mild reproof are generally sufficient. The older children, aware of their special responsibility in the class, and small enough in number to have positive recognition of the fact in special tasks and to be spared undue competition with each other, give an example that is at once helpful to the younger ones and satisfying to the teacher.

Teaching in Family-grouped classes is no easy assignment, but teachers seem to find in it the maximum satisfaction for their effort and a minimum of the more distasteful elements of punishment and tedious routine tasks.

Records

These possibly become more difficult to keep, as they are so highly individual. It has been suggested that they need to be of three types:

1. Records of individual achievement in the traditional skills. Normally kept by most class teachers, these note progress in reading and the consolidation of progressive steps in number. For the youngest children such records will be a mere indication of the fact that time has been spent by the teacher with them. "Attention to . . ." or a tick

---

[1] H. James and others: *Periods of Stress in the Primary School.*

[2] "Perceptive teachers are aware of the great power which they can wield through suggestion." A. Gesell and F. Ilg: *The Child from Five to Ten.*

followed by a few words on play or talk will suffice. Many comments have been made on the absolute necessity of keeping records of this kind with meticulous care. With so much variety in work and play going on, especially where the day is informal and a high degree of self-chosen occupation is permitted, children's academic achievement or non-achievement can easily be missed or passed over; individuals may not be given their due amount of attention.

2. Records of important happenings in children's lives, or indications of special temperamental traits. This kind of record keeps account of development or regression in areas of personality associated with emotional growth and character. It may record illness or accident, an unusually prolonged holiday or a stay with a relative at a time of domestic disturbance. It may record experiences which have caused emotional stress, such as the illness of a mother or a close friend leaving school, and it may refer to favourable social or emotional development or indications of special interest. For instance: "Paula N offered to help dress the little ones—first helpful act." "Donald P chose music again today—seems to have a flair—start him on a recorder?"

3. Class records. These are a routine matter, and list stories and poems told or read, songs and hymns learnt, class or group interests, movement introduced, gramophone records played, and so on. They are a necessary precaution against staleness, repetition or lack of variety.

None of the records described are difficult to keep, especially if the record books are always near at hand. Children's aid can be enlisted in some of the routine record-making. An older child will happily add the name of a newly told story to a list on the wall, or place another tick beside the name of a familiar one to show that, "We've had it four times now, and we still like it," as one 7-year-old said with satisfaction.

A similar technique can be adapted with "A Book of Songs We Know", or "Poems We Have Heard". Once the books are made the children do the rest, and are often the ones to remember and urge the teacher that the job needs doing. Handwriting may be imperfect, but the record is there and the class as a whole joins in the general interest.

In the same way, children can tick off on a chart their progress through a group of reading books. Provided that artificial rewards and stimuli (gold stars!) are not offered, and the teacher cultivates the general attitude that moving forward is the important thing and not who can move forward *fastest*, there will be no undue anxiety about who is getting on 'the best'. Fluent readers can keep a record of books read and even add a comment or two. This is another example of not doing for the children what they can do for themselves, and has the added advantage of furthering the children's involvement in their own learning.

It seems to be agreed that there is no place in the modern Infants' classroom for examinations and tests. In the words of a teacher: "We should know what each child can and cannot do. There is no point in testing him."

Role of the Headteacher

"There is gradually accumulating a vast amount of knowledge about children which is not yet fully used—for one obvious reason. Teachers are over-burdened. Classes are too large, and our duties and the outside calls on us expand every year; it is difficult (but not impossible) for us to find the time to sift and learn the newly discovered facts, to seek to verify them and to make experiments in basing our work upon them."[1]

How is the headteacher to use and help her colleagues to make full use of this growing knowledge? How can she ease the burdens of the staff and reduce pressures so that they may function better as teachers? How can she minimize the difficulties which sap physical and temperamental vitality?

First it is necessary to know the difficulties, to recognize the pressures that exist, and to be aware of the personal strengths and weaknesses of the team. The word 'team' is used advisedly, for the authors, in the course of this investigation, have been told many times of the feeling of kinship between colleagues in Family-grouped schools, owing to the fact that all now follow the same broad programme of work. Difficulties are not all the same, as all individuals differ, but all the teachers have common ground—the child from 4-plus to 7-plus.

Here is the first clue for the headteacher. In frequent, frank and free discussion, problems can be thrashed out and unity strengthened. Teachers themselves need new learning experiences; some are available near at hand and may be found in an interchange of ideas with colleagues. Discussion times keep teachers in touch with modern developments made available in books, talks or lectures. A special responsibility of the headteacher will be to arrange to free teachers for refresher courses, in-service training, or visits to other schools from which useful reports may be carried back to colleagues in school. Mewed up in their own classrooms, teachers are at a great disadvantage. They have little chance of knowing what is going on in other schools, or even in other classrooms in their own school. The first term of a year, in Family-grouped classes, when numbers are low, is an ideal time for teachers to make contact with other schools, other classrooms and other teachers.

---

[1] M. Brearley: *Studies in Education: First Years in School: The Practical Implications for the Teacher.*

The more teachers see and discuss, the more they clarify their own ideas and the more insight they develop. They grow in awareness of the importance of their own attitudes in provoking desirable responses from children. W. D. Wall[1] makes the point that it is vitally necessary for a teacher to understand herself and be aware of her own developing potentialities and her reasons for acting as she does. Although this is relevant to teaching at all ages, it probably has far greater significance at Infant level than at any other, as here the teacher plays a proportionately greater part in the child's learning and social experiences. Books and other teaching material have increasing impact as the pupil grows older; though the teacher's influence is always important it is never more so than at the Infants' stage. Sifting of experience through discussion can be very enlightening and the common experience of all the staff in the Family-grouped school provides a valuable basis for this.

Discussion also enables the staff to understand the programme and organization of the school as a whole and teachers are better able to assess their own part in the whole; the feeling is diminished that teachers and children are manipulated at administrative convenience rather than according to personal significance. If there is to be purposeful planning so that circumstances are as favourable as possible both for child *and* teacher, then teachers themselves must play a part in such planning. Several teachers have spoken of the new pleasure they have found in their work following discussion about the reorganization of the school into Family-grouped classes.

Such ways of helping teachers may seem nebulous. Are there more practical ways open to the headteacher? Many feel it as an absolute obligation to find ways to relieve them of every possible extraneous task which wastes their time and diverts them from their basic task of teaching.

Many Education Authorities provide ancillary Infant-helpers in their schools. Every teacher in turn should benefit in positive ways from their help in the classroom. According to the time available helpers can perform such routine classroom tasks as mixing paint, mending apparatus, washing pots and brushes, preparing clay, making paste, cleaning cupboards, attaching tapes, sharpening pencils and stapling and sewing books.

They can undertake such non-teaching tasks with children as playing number games, threading needles, paying attention to sick children, supervising groups in the playground, supervising cloakrooms or toilets, helping with clothing and mopping up.

Many tasks are performed by these valuable helpers which support teachers indirectly. But each teacher appreciates very much a share of

---

[1] W. D. Wall; *Education and Mental Health.*

personal assistance in the classroom, even though it be only perhaps once weekly.

Secretarial help now relieves teachers of time-consuming tasks in collecting dinner or stamp money. Ingenious schemes have been devised by headteachers so that class teachers are totally relieved of such tasks. Every moment spent by the teacher in attending to them reduces the time she could spend exercising her true function as a teacher.

The headteacher needs to be fully aware of the strengths and weaknesses of her teaching colleagues, and to take positive steps to pool the former and minimize the latter. The special talents of individual members of staff in music, arts and crafts, physical education and so on can be at the service of all, either in an advisory capacity or in some planned way. In at least one Family-grouped school, teachers take a special responsibility at planned times, in rooms organized to cater for children choosing to do music, physical education, arts and crafts, academic skills and domestic play. Children in other schools know that "Miss X is the teacher to go to if you want to find out about animals", or "Miss Y knows about music", or "Miss Z knows about making puppets". Thus individual talents are used throughout the whole school.

There are often good reasons for giving a teacher a slightly smaller class—the young and inexperienced, the older teacher near retirement, those undergoing stress in health or domestic matters. Having even half a dozen fewer children helps to relieve strain and the balance can be absorbed without undue inconvenience by other classes.

Many schools have the services of an extra part-time teacher, and these are used in varying ways; sometimes for remedial teaching, sometimes to relieve full-time members of staff, or to give help in many special ways, such as music teaching. The important thing is that the benefits be shared, and that *every* teacher feels the advantage of the addition to the teaching strength.

Many classes have special problems of accommodation, which the headteacher must seek to alleviate. The class in the sunless, north-facing classroom needs extra colourful equipment and pot-plants and extra time outdoors or in the hall. The children in the specially small room need to be fewer in number, to have access to extra playing space in corridors or cloakrooms and extra time in the hall. Furniture must be easily stackable. The teacher in the classroom without a sink needs two water trays (or a water tray and an old-fashioned zinc tub, with large jug and pail) and an extra time allocation of the Infant-helper to fill and empty them.

Classroom facilities are bound to vary in quality, especially in older, less well-planned schools. Compensations need to be found for small, dark or otherwise undesirable rooms.

In the same way it is evident that most headteachers feel an absolute obligation to take part wherever they can in the teaching and learning which goes on. Headteachers described to the authors with enthusiasm the varying parts which they play. As well as conducting the usual school worship, many also do the following:

1. Take classes of older children for music, story, hymn practice or Religious Education.

2. Work in classrooms with a teacher for some part of the day. One headteacher particularly mentioned the value of this kind of help for the insecure teacher who is perhaps new to Family Grouping.

3. Take groups of children from each class in turn for special attention to reading, number or written work.

4. Hear individual children read. This particular form of help was mentioned very often. The authors wonder whether there may be a danger of children coming to believe that the headteacher values reading more than any other aspect of school work.

5. Supervise groups in activities such as puppetry, painting, gardening and swimming.

6. Take over a classroom for a session or sessions so that the class teacher may be free to take a group on an expedition or visit another school.

All these activities bring the headteacher in close touch with the children and give opportunity for her special influence to be felt. This has special value for a class with a less able teacher, or one whose understanding is still limited.

There are problems of a general administrative kind for which preparation can be made. Foresight in organizing milk and dinner procedures, outdoor activities, cloakroom, washing and toilet routines, even the moving of children about the school in friendly groups rather than in over-organized quiet 'crocodiles'—all this saves time and temper. Headteachers and teachers have reexamined such routines and are eliminating the trivial repetitive activities which are time and energy consuming.

Every teacher can list them—the things she does over and over again, and the things she says over and over again. With large, constantly changing classes of dependent children, this is almost inevitable. It is one of the advantages of Family Grouping that such repetition is minimized.

In the foreseeable future it may be that teaching auxiliaries or assistants in every classroom will help to free teachers from some of the tedious detail of class organization so that every moment of the five hours a day which a teacher spends with the children can be most profitably used.

The authors felt it significant that so many headteachers wish to work closely in touch with children, and to watch with care the kind of use which they make of their opportunities. Such headteachers recognize, in the words of Sealey and Gibbon: "There must be an alliance of school practice with the natural growth pattern of children."[1]

We need to watch closely what a child actually *does* when faced with this material or that particular task. And having observed his response ask: "How can we use our own knowledge more effectively to supplement his response?" Teachers who do not think along these lines will dislike Family Grouping and are likely to fail with it. Those who do will grasp and enjoy the opportunities it offers—and find it easier than they anticipated.

---

[1] L. Sealey and V. Gibbon: *Communication and Learning in the Infants' School.*

8
Ways of Using Family Grouping

Transitional Family Grouping

In a Family-grouped class there will normally be children of the full age-range of the Infants' school. But by no means all Family-grouped schools are so organized.

In Bristol, for instance, 93% of the schools were in 1964 Vertically Age-grouped to some extent. Of these schools about one third had complete Family Grouping, whilst the remainder operated 'Transitional' Family Grouping, which was in some cases a stage towards full Family Grouping. In such schools 5 and 6-year-olds are grouped together, but the 7-year-olds are in separate classes. Some head-teachers feel that the 7-year-olds can be better catered for in a class of their own, and retain partial Family Grouping: others later move on to complete Vertical Age-grouping.

In some schools the older children are segregated because it is felt that children remaining in one class for the whole of the Infants' school period become too dependent on a single teacher. One head-teacher, recognizing the need for children to adjust themselves to a new situation when they enter the Junior school, firmly believes it is better for them to make the adjustment to a single-age class while still in the Infants' school. She said, "If you can make an adjustment in a known situation and come through it, then you have learnt something which will help you in life."

In this particular school the children come from very good home backgrounds and academic standards are above average. The head-teacher is of the opinion that if the 7-year-olds remain with the younger ones their progress will be hampered.

Another headteacher with experience of both Transitional and complete Family Grouping said, "Transitional Family Grouping is very good with children of high intellectual calibre. On the other hand these children are not necessarily mature in other ways; there is always the problem of a few older ones being left down." This headteacher preferred complete Family Grouping.

Some class teachers working with Transitional Family Grouping express the view that segregation of 7-year-olds is undesirable. They doubt whether the segregation of the older children does in fact provide any different preparation for the Junior school since the 7-year-olds, although in separate classes, still work informally. They give the following reasons for preferring full Family Grouping:

1. The main body of classes is left with a large proportion of the

youngest children, with only a few able to take responsibility or be a real asset to the class. The stimulus of the older children is lacking.

2. The main part of the classes consists entirely of the younger and middle age-groups, all demanding a great deal of attention at the same time.

3. These classes have to receive a greater proportion of new entrants than would otherwise be necessary, making absorption more difficult, particularly in the absence of the older children who can make the settling-in period so easy both for the children and the teacher.

4. Teachers lose the stimulus and interest of working with more mature children.

It could be added that unless there is a rotation of teachers every year (which it is hoped to avoid in Family Grouping) some teachers will never have the satisfaction of teaching the oldest children, and will have no opportunity of working with the whole Infants' school age-range. Likewise the teacher of the 7-year-olds will gain little or no practical knowledge of the development of the younger child.

On the surface it appears easier to provide greater intellectual stimulus where the children are all roughly the same age because the teacher can concentrate her efforts on the needs of this particular age-group, but it is doubtful whether more than a small minority will benefit from this. 40 children will always remain 40 individuals whatever their age. There is still a wide range of ability between them, calling for a continuation of individual and group methods of teaching. The most intellectually able children need to move on at their own pace and it is possible that the less able child suffers both intellectually and emotionally. Leaving him down in a class with younger children would be most discouraging; he might see himself as a failure. If he is allowed to go up with the other children of the same age as himself, he may still feel a failure since he will be more conscious of the progress of his peers than he would in a Family-grouped class. Thus one of the main advantages of Family Grouping—that of allowing a child to find his own level—is lost. Many opportunities for good social and emotional development will also be lost to both the older and younger children. Natural groups which have developed during the first one or two years of Infants' school life are broken up—particularly undesirable for those children who have little more than two years in the Infants' school and would only have about one year in each class. Such children will be called upon to make three adjustments to new situations in a period which can be as short as two years—from home to school, from class to class and from Infants' to Junior school. This is an unnecessarily heavy demand upon any child, however emotionally mature he may be.

Where Infants' and Junior schools are run separately children need a settling-in period when they first transfer from one to the other, irrespective of the type of organization to which they have become accustomed in the Infants' school. Junior teachers do not find that children from Family-grouped classes settle in less easily than those from Traditional classes. Some say that children from Family-grouped classes are more adaptable and ready for new experiences. This being so, there would appear to be little advantage in requiring children to adjust twice (i.e. from Family Grouping to age-grouping in the Infants' school, and then from Infants' to Junior school).

We came across one school in which the youngest group of children were separated from the others. The headteacher of this school considered that complete Family Grouping gave rather too wide an age-range, particularly as she was able to take in children under 5. In practice there was never a Reception class of completely new children, as a nucleus of the youngest children was always left behind, and there was always an established atmosphere. Similarly with the older children: about half the children remained each year to form the nucleus of the new class. The main object of this organization seemed to be to ensure that, whilst frequent changes of class were avoided, no child remained with the same teacher throughout his Infants' school life. Whilst this had many advantages over age-grouping, by placing together all the children who were ready for more formal work, there seemed to be unnecessary pressure on the teachers with the older children, and the younger children were unable to profit by the stimulus provided by the presence of the older children.

One other headteacher was at first hesitant about putting the Reception class children with the others. She said, "I thought they would not get sufficiently rich creative play—how wrong I was." This school now has complete Family Grouping.

The 'Cell' Class

In a very small number of schools one class has been organized on Family Grouping lines. This is sometimes experimental and sometimes a temporary expedient to meet a particular local need, such as a sudden influx of children of various ages due to housing development.

Administratively this seems to create no problems. In fact it can help stabilize the remaining classes by making it possible to avoid 'passing up' children in the middle as well as the beginning of the year.

On the whole parents like Family Grouping once they understand the reason for it (see Chapter 10), but where only one class is organized in this way it may seem a little strange to them. Some parents have the impression it is a special class for difficult or backward children. Others may regard it as an experiment (although the teacher may have worked along these lines for a number of years and no longer regard it as experimental). They wonder why, if it is considered successful, it is not extended to other classes.

Many of the advantages of Family Grouping arise from the very informal atmosphere of the Free Day. With such an organization the 3 Rs may be less apparent to parents, who naturally compare programmes and want to know why children in other classes are doing more formal reading and number work.

For these reasons the class teacher must spend more time explaining than would normally be necessary. A headteacher of a Junior Mixed and Infants' school said, "The structure of the whole school must be tuned to the Family Grouping idea, even if Family Grouping is not practised with the Junior children." This is even more true of a school catering for Infants only.

If all the teachers in a school are sympathetic to a Free Day with an informal approach, it is doubtful whether there would be opposition to Family Grouping. If they are not so tuned, then they are not tuned to the same approach to education.

Where the remaining members of the staff are not in favour of Family Grouping there is less common ground for discussion. Whilst a diversity of views can be said to add interest to the school, it can lead to the teacher of the one Family-grouped class feeling somewhat isolated, and to some extent losing the satisfaction of working as one of a team.

It is also possible that the children themselves may begin to feel they belong to an isolated unit and there is some difference between them and children in the other classes. Much depends on the particular school, and we did not in fact see this happening. In order to avoid this situation it is important to ensure that any privileges extended to children in the top classes should also be extended to the older children in the Family-grouped class.

Teachers' personalities vary a great deal, each having a different contribution to make to the life of the school. There must be ample scope for teachers to express their own individuality, but consideration must also be given to the extent to which it is desirable for the whole school to work within an agreed framework.

Rural Schools

In the last few years there has been a growing interest by urban schools in Vertical Age-grouping and many schools have chosen to adopt this form of organization.

It should not be forgotten, however, that the rural school has never had any choice and that the teacher in the village school has always had to provide for a wide age-range. This no doubt presented many difficulties when formal class lessons were the accepted method of teaching. Several very small groups would be together in the same room under one teacher whose task it was to divide her time equally between each group and ensure that none of the children wasted their time. No wonder the more 'fortunate' teacher in an urban school who had only to prepare one set of lessons for the whole class felt sympathy towards the rural school teacher.

With increased knowledge of the educational needs of young children, rural school teachers have taken the opportunity of their smaller classes to experiment with modern methods and a more individual approach. Much inspiring work has been done in such schools, and they have been an example to larger town schools in dealing with mixed age-groups. The village school and the nursery school have been the parents of Family Grouping.

One headteacher, after experiencing the advantages of a small village school, felt he was faced with a problem when the children in his urban school were organized into classes according to age. After reorganizing the school on Family Grouping lines he said, "Family Grouping was begun here from a knowledge of village schools and their advantages rather than a knowledge of any special movement."

But not all rural school teachers consider the mixed age-group to be to their advantage. In fact many such schools are still run on formal lines, obviously more difficult with a wide age-range. However, teachers seem to be well aware of other advantages which a small school offers. One teacher in a village school writes: "I would say that the small rural school has many advantages socially and emotionally. The teacher knows each child over a long period: the child develops as a whole person more easily than in a city school where children are perhaps streamed. The children's natural play facilities among animals, sand, water, trees, help emotionally, and being in the same class for 2 to 3 years they have social security. Brothers and sisters are a great help in settling younger children in a rural school."

In many country areas the village school has been part of family life for a number of generations. One rural school teacher with previous experience of town schools talks of the more active interest which parents (particularly fathers) seem to take in their children, "even taking time off from their work and travelling long distances to attend school functions. Village life is more intimate; the atmosphere of a rural school is more like an extension of this, and children fit naturally into the 'family' system. Family Grouping helps the rural children to feel more at home and more confident."

Physical conditions in many rural areas may fall far below those to be found in some city schools, and the very small school undoubtedly

A page from a "Personal Measurement Book"

I am going to be
a policeman

When I grow up I want to be a
teacher and I want to teach children
to write and to read and all sorts of
things that children have to learn
and teach them how to spell werds
and I will teach them how to make things
kathryn

Pages from a class book, "When I Grow Up", showing the contributions of children of 5 (top) and 6 years (bottom)

suffers many disadvantages, but the best of these schools show how well they can cater for the 'whole child', providing excellent opportunity for good emotional, social and intellectual development. Modern, well designed and well equipped rural schools probably give the finest early education available in this country today.

A number of the favourable views expressed in Chapter 10 have come from headteachers of small rural schools.

One teacher in a rural school with a class of 30 children aged 7 to 11 writes of the need to group children according to ability (i.e. not age) for efficiency in the teaching of tool subjects, but stresses the importance of allowing pupils of the same age to mix as much as possible, since "being permanently associated with pupils of younger years can have a discouraging effect on older scholars". This 'cross' grouping is, of course, one of the advantages of a Vertical Age-group. The teacher goes on to say that the children can undertake responsibility for the wellbeing of the younger ones: "A teacher's task in such a class is enormous and without the cooperation of the older children well nigh impossible to carry out well."

Some Junior teachers in rural areas are concerned that the family feeling experienced in the small school cannot be carried over into the large secondary school, but one teacher adds that "the self-discipline and initiative engendered may to some extent counterbalance this loss, although I am certain such children need careful and sympathetic handling for the first few months of Secondary school life."

Two other teachers in a small school where the intimate 'family' atmosphere is most marked think that their children going on to secondary schools were so self-confident and adaptable that they did not experience any difficulty. If children do find difficulty in settling down, they say, the fault is more likely to be with the Secondary school for not catering sufficiently for the individual. In their view the mixed age-group provides the ideal educational situation. On the other hand a headteacher writes: "I feel the children are perhaps less confident in new surroundings."

These remarks concern children in rural schools where there is no choice but to organize on Family-grouped lines. Schools large enough to make a choice are rethinking traditional organizations.

A headteacher of an urban school compared it with his former rural school where "there was little age-grouping at all throughout the whole school, and children gravitated to classes where they stayed three, four or five years". He loosened the organization of the urban one to encourage as much intermixing as possible of the various age-groups at all times. His aim was "to develop a community as distinct from a number of separate classes, the children of all classes being the concern of *all* the teaching staff". He also says: "Ideally I would like groups of 7–9 and 9–11 years.[1] I do not think a four-year grouping would be satisfactory owing to the vital changes in development around 9 years. When the numbers have stabilized and the 11-plus examination is abandoned I will organize the Juniors in two groups. Thus the primary child will spend its first seven years at school in three composite groups instead of seven separate 'quarantined' classes."

A headteacher of a Junior school of six classes has for five years arranged his pupils in "2 layers of 2 years" (i.e. 7 to 9 years, 9 to 11 years). The lay-out of his three-decker school (with Infants as a separate department on the ground floor) lends itself to a break at 9 years and this also seems to be in accord with children's natural development. It was found too that the former organization of streamed classes was producing undesirable social behaviour and problems in intellectual development.

Much thought needs to be given to the question of introducing Vertical Age-grouping into Junior schools, and it is interesting to note that the Department of Education and Science has encouraged experiment in this direction in the London experimental schools, Eveline Lowe and Vittoria.

Nursery Schools

A good Nursery school tries to provide the ideal environment in which children can grow and develop to their full capacity. Outside pressures concerning academic achievements which exist for a child of 5 entering the Infants' school are non-existent in the Nursery school, and this has left nursery teachers more free to experiment. They have been quick to put into practice the new knowledge which we now have of child development. As a result, a large proportion of Nursery classes have for many years been organized on Family Group lines.

Children of 2 and 3 years old are still very dependent on the adult for their physical requirements, and the teacher and her assistants need to be constantly at hand to meet the children's many demands. The child of 4-plus, on the other hand, is beginning to become a useful community member. Not only is he able to attend to many of his own needs without much help from the adult, but he is also eager to please and help. Where the ages of a group are mixed, the teacher does not need to spend so much time attending to the physical needs of the children, since the older ones are able to look after themselves to a considerable extent. In addition, the 4-year-old is well able to take responsibility, under supervision, for some of the routine jobs in the classroom, such as putting out toys or laying tables for dinner. He will also take pleasure in clearing up and seeing that everything is tidy. As

[1] See Chapter 11.

with the older child in the Infants' school, he has already been at the Nursery for some time and knows the routine.

New children fit in easily as they come along. The teacher is not faced with a group composed entirely of very immature children who have come away from their mother for the first time, all needing individual adult care. The presence of older children who are already secure and happy is a relief for the teacher in charge, and provides a stable atmosphere which the new immature children could not create for themselves. Thus the older children provide a sense of security for the younger ones, and in so doing develop feelings of responsibility.

In a Nursery school there is no direct teaching. The children develop in all ways by the many varied activities available to them and by imitation of the adult and the other children with whom they play. If the children are split into age-groups, the younger ones have little to learn from each other, whereas the comparatively mature 4-year-old is already beginning to have more contact with the outside world and will have stored up a fair amount of knowledge which he can share as he mixes with all the other children and enriches their play.

Perhaps one of the biggest advantages of Family Grouping in the Nursery schools is found in speech development. In the past when children were grouped according to age, language development tended to be very slow. The children playing together were equally immature in speech. With the mixed age-groups the younger children acquire from the older ones a richer vocabulary and clearer speech.

Advantages gained by Family Grouping in a Nursery school are similar to those gained in the Infant Department.

British Forces Schools

There is, of course, no basic difference between Forces and civilian schools, but teachers in Forces schools find in Family Grouping a solution to the problem of instability which is considerable where there is a shifting population. In answer to the question, "Why did you start Family Grouping?" one headteacher writes: "Constant enrolment of Infants throughout the term, steadily increasing roll, and termly admission of new entrants (always greater than in a normal school) were leading to constant and rapid movement from class to class. This, coupled with the rapid turnover of children and staff (normal in Army schools), was causing great instability under the traditional system."

Some of the other views expressed elsewhere (Chapter 10) are those of headteachers of British Forces schools in Germany, many of which are organized in Family Groups.

One headmaster writes: "It is clearly beyond our power to do anything about the basic problem (i.e. of the shifting Army personnel), but it behoves us at least to reduce movement within the school to a minimum." He describes such movement as "undesirably frequent", and gives an account of the measures taken to convert his school to a Vertically Age-grouped one.

"Many other advantages" were found to be gained. They are identical with those described elsewhere in this book.

9

Changing the Traditional Pattern

We need to cultivate an attitude of respect for each child: each one is a unique individual who matters. To push children about from class to class for administrative convenience is a negation of this attitude.

A Teacher.

No school is likely to undertake the change from Traditional to Family Grouping without careful thought. Rearranging a school already fully established in Horizontal Age-grouping can be profoundly disturbing and may not be successful. There are schools which have made the change, disliked the results and changed back again. There is at least one school which, having made the change, thought it unsuccessful and changed back again, then decided that after all Family Grouping was to be preferred, and reverted to it.

Many schools have found their own way to Vertical Age-grouping, sometimes without any awareness of the fact that it is a recognized 'system' at all. The authors find this profoundly significant. It indicates that, far from taking up a new educational trend as a 'gimmick' for the sake of its newness, or adopting a fresh theory about learning or child nature in order to keep in the forefront of educational practice, teachers and headteachers dissatisfied with the way in which traditional methods were working out *for the children they were teaching* decided to modify the old system in accordance with what they had found from first-hand experience to be the needs of children.

Here follow some accounts by headteachers themselves which describe old ways giving place to new.

First is an account by a headmaster about a new Junior Mixed and Infants' school:

"When the school opened in 1961 the classes were organized in the usual way, i.e. Reception, 6 years, 7 years, etc. At the end of the first term, I was shocked by the upheaval of putting beginners up and all the classes being seriously disturbed; but what impressed itself upon me most was the lack of drive and desire to learn and enjoy in all the Infant classes, especially the Reception group. My experience of Infants led me to expect a much livelier response to the learning stimulus."

The headmaster here refers in detail to his former experiences in a village school and goes on: "My Deputy and two of the Infant teachers had taught in village schools and understood what I meant by 'lack of sparkle' among the Infants, and agreed to a change. The only thing to do was to group the classes in complete age-groups as in village schools; thus we created three classes of 5 years to 7 years equal in every respect. Later this grew to five and now is four Family-grouped classes. It was not until we had been working in this way for about a term that I learned of the 'Vertical Grouping' movement.

"You may say that I stumbled across this by accident, but that is not strictly true, for I had observed the effects of age-mixing in a village school and in my mind there is no excuse for Horizontal grouping at all, for such organization is really anti-social.

"The organization is simple. Each class contains the whole Infant age-range. Beginners are admitted to each class in turn, efforts being made only to preserve equal distribution of the sexes. Only one child is admitted to a class at a time and has the attention of the teacher and the class for the whole morning or afternoon. This is usually long enough for the child to be absorbed into the class. Total integration, of course, takes longer, but the process is very quick; two or three days for most children.

"Mixing with older children and juniors is encouraged at all times. Children are encouraged to stay to school dinners (Family Service— run almost entirely by the children) where a great deal of mixing takes place. The whole idea is to develop a community as distinct from a number of separate classes."

Another headmaster describes his school adapting to meet a special need:

"Many experiments in organization and teaching techniques are introduced to meet difficult or peculiar conditions, and then become accepted practice because they are found to have special values of their own. The vertical classification of the Family Grouping system in use at —— School began in such circumstances.

"The school, opened in May, 1954, to serve a large new housing estate, was originally planned as a one-form Infants' and two-form Junior entry school. It soon began to experience the problems of overcrowding." (The headmaster describes accommodation difficulties as the school roll rose in four years to a peak of 674.) "The greatest difficulties were faced by the Infants' classes, and as the rates of admissions in 1957 and 1958 increased steadily to an average of 35 a term, it became necessary to delay the entry of children first for one term after their fifth birthday and then for two terms.

"This meant that some children were to spend only four terms in the infant classes. Moreover, without any spare room available it was necessary each term to make room for the next intake. It became increasingly clear that unless something could be done to provide conditions of greater security and stability, the progress of the youngest children, already handicapped by their late entry, would be further affected both socially and educationally.

150

"And so, by stages, the system of Family Grouping was introduced. The experiences gained during the difficult early years until the largest bulge moved into and through the Junior classes taught us such valuable lessons that this organization has been retained although the pressure of numbers has been reduced."

Another example of the valuable measure of stability which Family Grouping gives in special circumstances is brought out in the following description by the former Organizer for Infant Education in the Army schools in Germany:

"Children are in a constant stage of flux. They come from schooling in England to stay perhaps for a short period in the Reception area, then off again; parents are on the move; teachers are on the move; perhaps the children are moving up within a school.

"Family Grouping was introduced to give a measure of stability. The staff are mostly young, keen and enthusiastic. They like it. Now many schools have adopted it."

The headteacher of a school where Family Grouping has been long established looked back to the early days of the school, which had been built to serve a new housing estate:

"Attendance was appallingly bad. We looked into this and found that the children came to school best on the afternoon when we gave them free choice. So we gave them a free afternoon twice a week. Attendance promptly went up. So it was obvious, wasn't it? Soon we were working freely all the day. Family Grouping followed naturally. It is an essential adjunct to the Free Day. We never even think about attendance now. It's usually in the 90%s."

Yet another headteacher speaks of starting Family Grouping "because of an unusually large intake, and to obviate the necessity for transfers within the school throughout the school year."

Several headteachers describe the growth of the system in such terms as: "It just evolved to meet the needs of children and staff."

Another headteacher is more explicit:

"We grew into it. We started it in an attempt to harmonize temperaments between teacher and children. This gave a 12-month age-range in most classes, with a 24-month age-range across the two overlapping classes (i.e. 5 years/6 years: 6 years/7 years). Gradually we spread the 6's and 7's over five classes and then *on the staff's insistence* introduced the 5-year-olds."

The instances given above are all of individual schools meeting their own needs and finding their own solutions to situations which they had found unsatisfactory. As far as we are aware there is only one instance of major change taking place on an area basis—that which began in Bristol some 18 to 20 years ago.

Here a combination of factors operated, including a major building programme, an upsurge of new thinking about the most appropriate ways to educate young children, and the availability of a number of new headships. A study group considered the design of schools and planned the 'family' unit of classroom, play/work terrace, cloakroom and lavatory. The introduction of new and flexible ways of organizing children and staff included Vertical Age-classification which now operates in full or transitional forms (see Chapter 8) in 93% of the schools.

Preparation for the Change-over

Clearly it is much easier for a newly opened school, in the absence of an already established régime and tradition, to adopt Vertical Age-grouping.

What happens when the established school feels the need to make a change? How is it best to set about it? A great deal of thought, discussion and planning are needed well in advance of any projected change. 'Planning' is the operative word. At least one school is known to have thought, talked and prepared a year in advance. Their change went through without a hitch.

Such plans must include:

1. Allocation of classrooms: for varied sizes, appropriate variation in roll: time-table or other compensations for inadequate facilities in particular rooms (see page 137).

2. Allocation of children to particular teachers: schools have mentioned various ways of doing this, all giving individual teachers an opportunity to express preferences for children whom they already know, all stressing the need for considered discussion of children known to have learning or behavioural difficulties.

The school policy on members of the same family (to keep together or not) needs to be determined in the light of all pertinent facts about individuals, including the parental view.

Writing of the way in which the rearrangement of classes was dealt with, a teacher says:

"Our first task was to rearrange the children into their new groups. This was done first purely by age; i.e. roughly the same number of children of a particular age were put into each group. These groups were then slightly rearranged to make sure that brothers and sisters were together, and we also tried to avoid separating children who had already become close friends or who seemed to be of mutual help to one another. A few children who seemed to upset one another were deliberately separated. Children coming up from the Nursery class or other new entrants were added to the most appropriate class. Wherever possible parents' wishes were taken into account.

"After this initial regrouping only one or two changes were made as time went by. One instance of this was a girl of Junior age who was kept in the Infants' Department (of the Junior Mixed and Infants' school) because of backwardness due to poor health and a severe speech defect. It was felt that it would be better to separate her from her younger, brighter sister who was making good academic progress."

3. Sorting equipment: this is a major task and takes a long time. All classes need material and apparatus for use at all levels but in smaller quantities (see Chapter 2). Fresh major equipment (e.g. sand and water trays) may have to be provided; Local Authorities will sometimes allocate an allowance for this purpose. Books are not normally a problem, as they are frequently kept in a common central store from which teachers select at need. It is sometimes possible to treat a common stock of small apparatus in the same way.

4. There is need for discussion on a general policy for keeping records (see Chapter 7).

5. General agreement on the daily programme is necessary. Upon the basis of common agreement there is bound to be much variation with teachers of differing backgrounds, interests and experience. A degree of common agreement may often be obtained by arranging a visit for each teacher to another school where Family Grouping is in operation. As it is often particularly difficult to release Infants' teachers for this purpose, this is a further reason for long-term planning.

"We were able to visit a school," says one teacher, "where Family Grouping was already being carried out. We came back very impressed and anxious to start in our own school. The visit was followed by much discussion, and eventually plans were made to start after the Summer holiday."

Plans should also include arrangements for review and discussion after the change has been made.

6. Arrangements for informing parents: these are of the utmost importance. Upon the efficacy of the home-school communication may depend the quality of parent-teacher cooperation for some time to come.

A headteacher describes the steps which she took to explain the proposed change to parents:

(a) "A letter was drawn up summarizing the new plans, and showing clearly the difference between the old and the new organization. At the appropriate time it was sent to all parents of children already in school and copies were reserved to give to parents new to the school when their children entered, as they would almost certainly be expecting the traditional system remembered from their own childhood.

(b) Parent-teacher meetings were held in which organization and methods of teaching were explained and discussed. Such explanations were always warmly appreciated. It transpired that many parents were puzzled by modern methods but were often too diffident to question teachers.

(c) There was a general policy of an 'ever-open door' for parents. If they called to see the headteacher they were never refused; difficulties were willingly discussed. There was no objection to their walking about the school as they wished, and an anxious mother might spend part of a morning or so in the classroom with a new entrant. The same attitude of free access was maintained with regard to the class teacher, with the commonsense proviso that she should not be expected to give time to talk while occupied with the class, but would make an appointment for some more convenient time.

This policy of free access to staff and classroom was very seldom abused and greatly facilitated home-school cooperation." (There are schools which keep a special notice-board for messages to mothers. In others mothers invited to make suggestions for ways of helping 'their' school have formed themselves into groups to help with the making of apparatus, to do simple toy mending or sewing, to collect savings stamp money and to escort children to and from minor ailments' clinics. Some have asked to be allowed to 'hear' reading and have not been refused.)

An uninvolved onlooker attended a meeting of parents at which the proposed reorganization was under discussion and wrote:

"It was explained to parents that:

(a) Brothers and sisters would be together in the same class. This is a point which definitely appeals to most parents when a new child is brought to school. They are pleased if it can join a brother or sister, as they realize that school is a strange world for a five-year-old coming straight from home, and they know that the presence of a sibling will be some comfort to the child and will help to settle him down.

(b) Family Grouping removes the necessity to pass from one class to another in the middle of a child's Infants' school life or even in the middle of a school year. In this connection it was pointed out that any change in classes is bound to cause some regression in the child's work and it was the school's aim to avoid such unnecessary changes.

(c) The teacher becomes acquainted with the whole family and has a fuller knowledge of the home background. She is therefore in a better position to help if difficulties arise.

(d) A new child has time to become accustomed to the classroom before being required to play a significant part himself. In a Reception class he can only see other children who are feeling strange and insecure themselves. He learns from watching older ones at work. He is also helped in little personal tasks such as undressing and dressing for P.E.

(e) Even when children in one class are roughly the same age, there is still a wide range of ability. An Infants' teacher always has to treat her children as individuals, and cannot teach effectively more than a small group at a time.

It was emphasized that the five-year-olds would not be expected to do work too difficult for them and that the seven-year-olds would not be held back by the presence of the five-year-olds.

More individual help could be given to smaller groups requiring formal teaching of the skills."

7. As far as possible, the *children* should understand the changes that take place in their own little world. The younger children accept change without much question, but older ones can sometimes be confused, or even a little worried by the fact, for instance, that they are now being taught in the room they have known as 'the baby room', or the 'bottom class'. They do also sometimes ask why they have not 'gone up'.

Frequent reassurance in the early stages of the change-over that all classes are 'the same', backed by simple devices such as a card on each classroom door bearing the teacher's name followed by "Children of 5, 6 and 7 years old" soon overcome doubts, and in a very short time the old system of horizontal classes with their 'going up' routine is forgotten.

It is essential that the children themselves should be reassured, as they are the mouth-piece of school affairs at home; a confused or anxious 7-year-old can give parents some distressing moments.

8. Lastly, it must be recognized that, the change having once been made, both children and teachers need time to settle in before they can produce their best work.

The headteacher has a very special function at this time to alleviate anxiety, to draw upon herself, by discussion and a permissive attitude, parental or other complaints, to act as a safety valve for teachers contending with day-to-day difficulties and to reassure by the tolerance of her attitude those who take time to adapt and who may not at first achieve the measurable results for which they would normally look.

"Children can help themselves only if they are allowed to do so." This remark in Chapter 3 does not imply suddenly releasing children used to a rigidly teacher-controlled classroom to do what they will, in company with others of mixed ages. That way lies disorder—even disaster—and a rapid return to a more highly organized Horizontally-grouped school.

That is how not to do it.

10

A Variety of Views

The proof of the pudding is in the eating.

Old Saying.

The authors considered it important that this book should be based on the experience and opinions of teachers. To this end they have made as much personal contact as possible with teachers working on Family Grouping lines. Questionnaires have been answered frankly by many headteachers. Much personal contact has also been made with parents of children in Family-grouped classes, and questionnaires were sent to parents of children in one school. Children's own views have not been neglected, although it is appreciated that these may be of slight significance, owing to a child's inability to make a comparison. Adverse views are presented wherever they have been expressed.

The success or failure of any teaching method or type of organization is ultimately dependent on the skill and personality of the individual class teacher; a good teacher will make a success of any method provided she has confidence in it. Many teachers who have not had experience of Family Grouping or who have given it only superficial thought dismiss it as just one more new idea in education which would only add to their already heavy burden. It is encouraging, therefore, to note the wholeheartedness with which teachers in charge of Family-grouped classes express their enthusiasm.

It was found that although, as one teacher said, "It doesn't solve all the problems", the majority of teachers were fully in favour of it and were eager to list the many advantages they had found.

Teachers' Views: Effects on Themselves

Critics of Family Grouping often assert that it adds to the strain on the teacher, and in fact one teacher of a mixed age-group did say, "It is a far greater strain on a teacher's ability and much more strenuous." It would seem, however, that it is the informal approach as opposed to formal teaching which calls for so much strenuous effort on the part of the teacher. These freer methods, with the need for a great deal of individual attention, do make heavier demands on the teacher than more formal class lessons, but teachers find that with a mixed age-group it is easier to make full use of informal methods. They find they are more able to work towards their educational ideals.

One group of teachers wondered "how on earth we managed with classes of children all the same age". Another teacher, having worked with a mixed age-group, found it extremely difficult, on transferring to a Traditionally-grouped school, to meet all the needs of a class of 6-year-olds.

Most teachers felt that there were advantages for the teacher as well as the child, and the following views illustrate the points which appeal to them:

"Less pressure from the middle group just off with their reading. Always responsible children available in the class."

"Teachers can start with small classes in September, building up through the year, and therefore can make a more detailed study of the needs of each child."

"Less time is spent by the teacher in explaining class routine to the younger children, since this is absorbed by imitation and emulation of the older members."

"I find it easier to give adequate attention in the basic skills to the older children. Standards are higher."

"Easier to give more individual attention when one has smaller groups than teaching a class all at the same time; every child is working by himself while the teacher is taking a group or an individual child."

An elderly (highly skilled) teacher said, "You never get a class full of big rampageous boys."

There are Infants' schools in which teachers remain with the same age-group year after year, and are thus denied the opportunity to gain insight into the children's full development. Where teachers go up with their classes they become more conversant with the needs of the child from 5 to 7 years, and can take a responsible attitude towards the school as a whole. Teachers in Family-grouped schools welcome the opportunity to have the full Infants' school age-range before them at the same time so that they are aware of the continuous progress made by the children. Progress, which would be hardly perceptible in a class where the children are all of the same age, becomes much more apparent when it is seen side by side with that of younger children; and as one teacher said, "Working with children of all ages is much more intellectually satisfying for the teacher." Asked what she felt appealed most to her staff, one headmistress wrote: "The different age-range gives tremendous variety—no chance of boredom."

Comments on this point were so frequent that it is clear that teachers themselves feel the need for intellectual stimulus. The following are typical:

"There is a great pleasure in watching the gradual development of a child in the two years he is with the teacher. There is so much for us to learn from the children in that time."

"I particularly enjoy the continuity of it."

Many teachers have made reference to children's heightened sense of responsibility and pleasure in *their* work and *their* classroom. One teacher said: "The children take over the classroom." Another teacher wrote: "It gives the older children a chance to be responsible and kind." And another: "There is a real community spirit and 'family' feeling with everyone helping each other rather than competing."

Atmosphere

One aspect of Family Grouping frequently mentioned is this natural 'family' atmosphere which makes transfer from home to school easier. The following quotations are selected from the questionnaires sent to headteachers:

"I feel Family Grouping is simply an extension of the home, and there is no simpler or more natural way of making the dramatic change from home life to school."

"It is more of a life situation with a two-way flow—security from the home extended to the school, and of course the other way round."

"The atmosphere of haste is eliminated."

"A lively contented atmosphere is created."

Effects on Children

Teachers talked and wrote a lot about the ways in which children profited from Family Grouping. The following are some of their views:

"Children are more involved with their own progress."

"I hope the children will *think* for themselves and develop a keen attitude to learning and living."

"There is always someone in the class who is more competent or less competent: so everyone can do something."

"In Nature Study expeditions to the seashore and the woods Family Grouping works wonderfully."

"The fear of being 'bottom of the class' is greatly reduced or eradicated."

"I have often been asked whether the (smaller) children learn anything by being with the older ones, and the answer is 'yes, and more quickly'."

"Ready integration of newcomers."

"No sense of inferiority (or superiority) with other classes."

Disadvantages

Many teachers, asked for disadvantages, said: "I find none." One headteacher replied: "We discussed and overcame these so long ago I cannot remember them now." Another teacher said: "Of course there are disadvantages, but in my opinion they are counterbalanced by the

158

social give and take." One headmaster of a Junior Mixed and Infants' school, after listing many reasons why he thought the form of organization valuable, concluded: "I don't think there are more problems with this method—some different ones probably, but we think it very worthwhile!"

A teacher said: "The problems are different—no more than in a class with children of one age-group, who are often in as many stages socially and mentally."

Some said they found difficulty with class lessons such as story and music. Most teachers had discarded the formal news period in favour of informal group conversations. None of the teachers felt the difficulties were insurmountable.

With the modern approach to Physical Education, this lesson does not seem to present difficulties to most teachers. In fact, one head-teacher of a rural school who had previously taught in an urban area said: "Family Grouping in Physical Education has proved itself successful and enjoyable for everyone concerned."

Some of the other disadvantages mentioned are:

"It is difficult for another teacher to take over the class, especially for short periods."

"Where a free timetable is impossible because of the sharing of a building and playgrounds, the scope of Family Grouping is limited."

"Where two or three teachers on the staff are specially gifted, musically or artistically, only a small proportion of the children in the school get the full benefit of their talents."

"Brighter top Infants are perhaps not stretched as much as they might be in a normal class. Difficult for teacher to get sufficient time with small groups. Larger amounts of equipment required owing to duplication within rooms."

In a school with only one class Family-grouped for a short period, the headteacher said: "I think the 6-year-olds get the biggest advantages—they have the best of both worlds. But I am not so sure about the 5 and 7-year-olds".

Answers to more specific questions showed that on the whole teachers do not find it difficult to organize the daily programme so as to ensure that adequate attention is given to each age-group, although a few did say there was a tendency to devote too much time to the older children.

One teacher said: "These tendencies are similar to those experienced in Traditionally-grouped classes, for where classes are too large for adequate attention to be given to every child, teachers' personal sympathies are bound to affect the proportion of time devoted to the various groups, whether they are based on intelligence or age. The important thing is for teachers to be aware of these dangers."

Asked whether the younger children are a nuisance to the older ones, or whether the older ones spoil the work and play of the youngest, one teacher said: "Some older children begin to be resentful of younger ones wanting to be with them, 'tagging along'," but this view was not shared by other teachers. The more general view was that: "The younger ones are not in any way a nuisance to the older ones, nor do the older ones spoil the play of the younger children."

Standards of Work

Naturally teachers are concerned about standards. Most find that the older children stimulate the younger ones in their work, and that on the whole younger children are not worried by the standards of the older children. One teacher did, however, say: "Some younger children become disturbed when they see the work of the older group, and are afraid of being expected to do the same—some become disturbed because they are unable to compete and want to be as good."

It is difficult to judge accurately how standards reached in a Family-grouped class compare with those in an Age-grouped class. We can only quote from what headteachers have said in reply to the question: "Do you consider that the academic attainments of the children in a Family-grouped class compare favourably with those for children in a Horizontal Age-group?"

"Yes, but of course I am speaking only of a school with an informal approach."

"The rate of learning is much increased. (May be a doubtful advantage?)"

"In July, 1964, I sent a group of 70 children up to the Junior school, and those who had been in a Family-grouped class and had been encouraged to work individually were far more mature, capable and sure of their knowledge and attitude to learning than those who had been in a class where the teacher had worked formally with a small age-group: the difference was most marked, and the Family-grouped children were academically in advance of the others, although I am sure all the children possessed an equal potential."

"Yes; in fact where teaching is good and stimulating and caters for children's needs, attainments are higher than usual."

"Subjective judgments indicate improved performance all round. Reading particularly benefits. This is the staff view and that of an H.M.I. who observed the classes recently."

A teacher of many years' experience of formal teaching said: "Oh yes . . . the 7-year-olds work just the same—only more so." Many teachers and headteachers merely said "Yes".

Finally, the following extract from a report of the Reading Education Committee sums up:

"Results in the Infants' school are difficult to assess in any event; comparison of one system with another is well nigh impossible. We can only say that for our children educational progress under this organization seems better than under another, and that the greater feeling of security which the children derive from the continuing care of the same teacher and the same familiar classroom environment is clearly reflected in their greater independence and increased capacity for responsibility."

Headteachers Assessing Difficulties for Staff

Headteachers were asked the question: "If you have inexperienced teachers on your staff, do you consider that the Family Group presents them with more problems than a class grouped according to chronological age? Some of the answers were:

"Yes, young teachers are not aware of what each age-group is capable of."

"Inexperienced staff sometimes find it difficult to organize."

"This should not present a problem, as even in a class grouped chronologically the children would be at different stages because of ability. Family Grouping is only an extension of this."

"I had a 'first appointment' teacher, a teacher returned to full-time after 19 years, and another after 2 years. They found it bewildering at first, but within 2 weeks had settled down into their stride."

"All teachers, however long they have taught, appear inexperienced when they first start Family Grouping. The ability to cope successfully with Family Grouping appears to lie in the attitude towards it more than actual teaching experience. Young teachers with only 2 years' experience have managed excellently, while others with between 6 to 15 years' have failed to understand even the rudiments of it. Consequently it is unfair to the children and teacher for their class to be Family-grouped."

"Definitely not. The system is a challenge to the teacher's training, and many have commented that Family Grouping allows them to teach in the way they were taught at college. It is reasonable to suppose, therefore, that the young teacher should feel more at home with these groups. The difficulties occur with the experienced teachers who have never been allowed to teach properly since they left college. However, like most late converts, when they realize the many advantages they really become quite fanatical about it."

"Teachers who have not had village school experience find great difficulty at first, but so far none have wanted to revert to Horizontal Grouping."

"The young teachers have sometimes been more at home with the method than experienced ones."

"My staff is a mixture of old and young, with varying experience, talents, and weaknesses. They all love it."

L

Rooms and Equipment

Many teachers stress the need for large classrooms for Family-grouped classes. Others say that by careful planning, they can run their classes successfully in small rooms. One Headteacher says: "In small rooms staff should be prepared to jettison furniture in order to make a play area, a large quiet corner, etc., and display apparatus—e.g. reserving part of the room entirely for number activity."

More than one headteacher made this comment:

"We have found it a great advantage to dispense with the more traditional arrangement of an Infant room. Classrooms have been arranged almost in sections, and use has been made of lockers, bookshelves, etc., to partition off and arrange rooms more attractively, and in the interest of greater efficiency."

Teachers New to Family Grouping: Formal v. Informal Methods

Where teachers have had no experience of Family Grouping, opposition to the idea often stems from lack of conviction about informal methods of teaching rather than the actual mixing of age-groups. Frequently they will say that they do not like the idea of having to provide for free-choice activities throughout the day for the immature children while the older ones are working. They tend to doubt whether they could provide adequately for the wide age-range.

A headmaster comments: "Two of the staff would prefer conventional grouping, but they would also prefer a formal atmosphere."

A number of teachers, interested in, but not entirely in favour of, Family Grouping, have said that they like the idea of always having some older children in the class able to cope with some of the classroom 'chores'.

Teachers are also quick to appreciate the advantage of not having to 'pass children up'.

"Passing up seems a waste of time—it may take a month for a teacher really to get to know a child's capacity, and for the child to adjust to the new group."

Once teachers have tried Family Grouping most of them enjoy teaching in this way. "I'd never done this before. For half a term I was completely at sea. Now I wouldn't change for anything."

"Now I am in a Family-grouped school I can teach for the first time as I was trained to do at college."

One might wonder whether inexperienced teachers find difficulty in a Family-grouped class. One such teacher (who has since had experience of Traditionally-grouped classes) says: "Group work in a Family-grouped class in the 3 Rs is just as easily organized and taught as in an ordinary class. Difficulties of teaching the 3 Rs are often given as a reason against Family Grouping, but, from my

162

limited experience, I don't find this criticism actually justified. I should think most young teachers going into Family Grouping from college would enjoy it once they'd got used to it."

Other Views from Teachers
"A mother is less anxious, a teacher is less harassed, and above all the child does not feel completely *alone*."

"Boasting, annoyance with 'slower' children, laughing at 'dim' ones, etc., which some 6 and 7-year-olds begin to indulge in (in ordinary classes) seem absent in a Family-grouped class."

"Tears are few."

"There is never any problem with discipline."

"Toilet training and handwashing are taught by example."

"Horizontal streaming appears no matter how we dislike it. Some children learn more quickly than others. Bright children irrespective of their age can work together, and so can others who for some reason or another feel anxious and need more time."

"We are really feeling the benefit this term. I feel that the problems posed by Family Grouping are no greater than in any other organization, and are more easily overcome in that they are more clearly revealed. One is compelled to face individual differences, and not to gloss over them."

"When colleagues talk to me of the Reception class I feel they are speaking of the crinoline!!"

Parents' Views
Parents of children in the Infants' school often have very little idea of what really goes on there, particularly when their child is a first 5-year-old. Generally they are only aware of whether he appears to have settled down happily or not. If a child is not happy about school he will probably not be able to give any specific reason for this, and disturbed behaviour at home or reluctance to go to school may be the only signs that all is not well.

A parent's image of school is usually that built up in his own school days, with scanty knowledge of the changes which have been taking place in recent years. The general picture is of class teaching (or at best group lessons), and it is difficult for them to imagine the individual work which goes on in a modern Infants' school. Sometimes their first reaction to Family Grouping is: "How can my child of five possibly keep up with the older children in the class?" Or: "How can my child of seven make satisfactory progress when there are so many younger children in the class?" Parents are afraid that their children's education (progress in the basic skills) will suffer. For this reason, particularly where Family Grouping is new in the school, it is important constantly to explain what is being done. Provided this reassurance is given they will be content when they realize their child has settled down well to school routine. As time goes on, they like to have the satisfaction of knowing he is making the normal progress which could have been expected in a class organized on traditional lines.

Only a very small minority of parents express disapproval of Family Grouping once the settling-in period is over. In the majority of these cases the disapproval is occasioned by misunderstanding, and a short explanation of the organization is usually sufficient to satisfy the parent that his child's best interests are being served. The only other adverse criticism arises when a child is not making progress in his work, through lack of innate ability or for some other reason. The former is often difficult for a parent to accept, and it is only too easy to blame the school, however organized, for lack of progress. It is probably true to say that many parents are not greatly concerned with the organization of the school, provided their children are happy and making reasonable progress.

In practice, a large number express enthusiasm for Family Grouping. Mothers bringing young children to school for the first time are generally relieved if there is an older relative or friend in the class to take care of them. When mother and child have come to know the teacher through older children, rapport is already established. One teacher remarked:

"Parents have confidence in the teacher they already know when the second or third child is admitted. When they see the good results of Family Grouping they are pleased; they feel that the teacher is their friend."

A few mothers wonder whether siblings will disturb each other through quarrelling, but as sibling rivalry seems to diminish in school, such anxiety is quickly alleviated. Most mothers are only too pleased for their children to be together, and frequently say so. One mother wrote: "I find that Family Grouping is just right for Barbara and John. With only one year between them they have always been together in everything. John, being the younger, looked to Barbara for a lead in most things. Being together in the same class they are able to talk together about things they do during the day, and, of course, they know the same children. My husband and I both think that they have got on very well with the school work, and they both like to learn in their own right. I still feel that being together has made a great difference, and I'm glad they had the chance."

Another parent with only one child in school wrote: "When children are so small, it is encouraging for them to be with older children. It's like being taken care of by an elder brother or sister."

Two mothers of girls who had spent their first year in a Traditionally-grouped class felt that their daughters were happier and had become more confident since joining a Family-grouped class. This was obviously due in part to greater maturity, but both were in fact very timid and the opportunity to care for younger members of the class gave them great satisfaction and helped to make them aware of their own greater maturity, which in turn helped them to achieve self-confidence. The mother of one of these girls said that her daughter had previously felt that she could not keep up with the rest of the class because she was slow to learn and lacked confidence, and that with younger, less able children in the same class she did not feel 'such a dunce'. The little girl was in fact far from being a 'dunce', but had begun to feel that she was one, because through lack of confidence she had felt unable to compete with other children of her own age. By the end of her Infants' school career she was still very timid, but her academic attainments were above average for the school.

The second girl, of very high intelligence, was very shy and withdrawn on entering the Family-grouped class at the age of 6. By the time she left the Infants' school she had achieved an extremely good relationship with both children and adults, and had become one of the most popular members of her class. On many occasions the mother expressed her appreciation of the class organization which she firmly believed had been the main factor in helping her child to overcome her shyness and enabling her to develop her intellectual ability.

It is at the 6-year-old stage that a minority of parents express concern that their children have not yet mastered the art of reading or formal manipulation of figures. Some of these parents wonder whether the teacher's time is taken up by the oldest and youngest children in the class, resulting in the neglect of the 6-year-olds.

Where specific teaching is delayed until about the sixth year it is perhaps inevitable that some anxiety will be felt by those parents who expect formal instruction in the basic skills to start as soon as the children enter school. Blame for the apparent lack of progress may be placed on Family Grouping. It is encouraging in these instances for both parents and children to be able to compare the attainments of a 6-year-old with those of a 5-year-old. One mother put this into words by saying: "He likes to know he can do harder work than the smaller children."

Open Days and other informal gatherings help parents to become aware of the considerable difference between the development of their 6-year-old and the 5-year-olds in the class. Many parents remark that they hadn't realized how much their child had achieved.

This period of uncertainty is usually short, as most children make fairly rapid progress once they reach the right stage of maturity for mastering the basic skills. One mother, typical of others who had previously expressed concern, a few weeks later said: "She seems to be getting on well now, although at first I did not think that she was making any progress, being in a class with all different ages."

The mother of an only child admitted that she was a bit doubtful at first, but after her little boy had been in school for two terms she was very pleased with the arrangement and felt that Family Grouping made it easier for an only child to mix with children both older and younger than himself.

The following two answers to questions put to parents are the only ones expressing discontent with their children's education. The first is about two brothers:

"Although I do think that Tony did familiarize Joey with his teacher and the activities of the Infants' school, I do not entirely agree that the mixing of age-groups is a good thing educationally."

"I can't possibly see how a child can further her education with three different groups of children doing three completely' different forms of lessons in one class."

Other parents wrote as follows:

"I think all children like to copy their seniors. I think learning that way comes more naturally. In my view Family Grouping is a very good idea."

"At first we were worried about Jean, being in a class with older children—if she would have the same teaching as in a class of all the same age, but she seems to have settled in and I have now seen her book which has put my mind more at ease, and her reading is coming along nicely and she seems to be happy."

"I think that Family Grouping is a great idea, as the younger children will probably learn a lot better and quicker. I think it will also help them to overcome any complexes they might have."

"I haven't any complaints and I am altogether satisfied. It is a very good idea and has worked wonderfully well."

"I am pleased with the way Richard has learnt to write and his reading is coming along well."

"I am all for the idea of a Family class and feel it is a great help for all future children who will be starting school."

Children's Views

Infants' schools nowadays are happy places to which children go willingly, and the unhappy child in school is the exception. Many express regret when the holidays come round. A child's happiness in school depends primarily on his relationship with the teacher and with other children. Provided the teacher is kind and understanding, organization or methods of teaching have little significance to him; his limited experience makes it impossible for him to compare them with any other type of organization or method. One cannot therefore attach much importance to views expressed by children on

Family Grouping, particularly as young children in their anxiety to please the adult will often say what they think is expected of them, and it is difficult to frame questions which will avoid this.

In a school where one class was Vertically Age-grouped and the remainder of the classes were grouped on traditional lines, some of the 7-year-old children from the top class who were known to have friends in the Family-grouped class were asked if they knew what was the difference between their class and the Family Group. All the children gave such replies as, "There is a hamster in that room," or, "There is a sink in that class." No child mentioned the different ages of the children, and when they were reminded of this they attached little or no importance to it. When questioned about it they thought they would enjoy having younger children in the class with them. Those with brothers or sisters all said they would like to have them in the same class. Beyond this they were unable to express any views.

In the same school, for the summer term it was found expedient to place about four or five new entrants in each class irrespective of the age-range of the existing class, so that for one term, owing to pressure of numbers, there was a modified form of Family Grouping in each class. A number of children from the top class were asked what they thought about this. None of the children considered that the little ones were in any way a nuisance to them: in fact they all obviously enjoyed having them, saying that "they played nicely" and "did not make a lot of noise". All the 7-year-olds said they like looking after the 5-year-olds and helping them to do their writing. One rather difficult, aggressive boy seemed to gain much satisfaction from adopting a kindly and protective attitude towards one of the new children. The older children were also pleased to have the opportunity to play with sand and water that had been brought in for the younger ones.

The children in the Family-grouped class were all well aware that their class was organized differently from the others, and without exception were full of enthusiasm for the mixed age-group. The 7-year-olds obviously derived great satisfaction from their sense of responsibility towards the little children. In all cases their attitude towards them was kindly and protective and in no way domineering. They said they liked helping them and enjoyed having them to play with. One boy of very low intelligence particularly enjoyed helping little children with their reading, little realizing how much he was helping himself. Most of the 7-year-olds said that they had their own special friends among the children of the same age as themselves, but all said that they had made friends among the younger children with whom they liked to play frequently. None of the children felt that the younger ones hindered them when they were working.

The younger children were unable to express any clear views on the organization of the class, but they did seem to appreciate that the older children on the whole were helpful to them and nearly all said they liked playing with the older children.

In presenting these views the authors acknowledge with gratitude once more the willing and frank cooperation of those closely involved in Family-grouped school life who have answered questions and stated their own opinions.

11

Vertical Classification in the Junior (Middle) School

> *We know that individual differences in maturation, both in speed and manner, cannot be eliminated, or even much altered; they can only be met by an educational system of great flexibility, a system based on a network rather than on a production line.*[1]

The class grouping of children of Junior school age is organized in a variety of ways by different schools.

The Plowden Report[2] lists and discusses five main ways of grouping (other than that of the one-class school), all of which fall into the broad categories of:

homogeneous streaming (by ability and sometimes by age)

non-streaming (heterogeneous ability grouping)

vertical streaming (ability grouping across year groups)

It is important to appreciate that the last of these types, *vertical streaming*, has nothing whatever to do with *vertical classification*, which is familiarly known in Infants' schools as Family Grouping.

Vertical streaming is the separation of brighter and duller children into classes which often draw from two or more year groups.

Vertical classification is the organization of children of all abilities (non-streamed), into mixed-age groups. The grouping is very flexible, and can consist of children of any ages which fall most conveniently together. It is the antithesis of streaming, either by age or ability.

The problem of how to group the children in a manner conducive to their maximum development, and at the same time keep the teaching situation comparatively simple is no easy one to solve. The Junior school is in a more favourable situation than the Infants' school in that it has only one intake per year, its numbers thereafter remaining virtually stable. But it does face the difficulty that ages, abilities and other relevant considerations, instead of clustering neatly in packages of thirty-six or forty, thereby making distribution into classes a comparatively simple matter, tend to group in patches through the four Junior school years, posing difficulties in class organization which can be very awkward administratively.

---

[1] J. M. Tanner: *Education and Physical Growth.*
[2] *Children and their Primary Schools*: Volume 2.

Whatever form of organization is adopted, some overlap is bound to occur. In ability streaming, the less able child in the 'A' stream may be surpassed by the most able in the 'B' stream.[1] Age distribution may be so irregular that some children may find themselves being promoted by a leap, too early, into an age group above their own, while others may have to be kept back to mark time at some stage in their Junior school life, because of an overlarge class. In the annual exercise of promotion, much of a headteacher's time and thought is consumed in reshuffling age and ability groups so that fair opportunity is given to each child and teacher.

Many heads and teachers are dissatisfied with the systems of grouping they settle for, particularly as childrens' abilities fluctuate and transfer may result in 'A' children dropping back into 'B' streams. They often feel uneasy, too, about pupils who they feel would benefit from a longer stay with a given teacher, but who are moved on by the inexorable machinery of 'passing up'.

Unhappily, the rigid structure of the 'standards', based on the Lowe Code of 1862, and initially on 'payment by results', still holds the majority of Junior schools in an inflexible and obsolete grip. The force of tradition is strong, and it has been reinforced by the 11 + selective system. For many schools the organization is self-perpetuating, heads and teachers being perhaps not fully aware of other possibilities.

The village and small rural school must perforce contain classes where age-groups cover more than one year. Viewed through the eyes of tradition this may seem to be a disadvantage. But many such schools are liberal and progressive in outlook, offering a sound education based on individual development, mutual help and self-discipline. Some larger schools have looked at them, and have looked again, at the philosophies involved in the practice of annual transfer and re-organization (whether based on ability or not) and have rejected them as the basis for their own organization. They are questioning whether these practices produce the most satisfactory environment in which young children can develop their innate abilities, learn new skills and acquire a body of knowledge which is coherent because rooted in first hand experience and cultivated by continuity of teaching. Schools are coming round to believing that "expectation based on chronological age classifications by I.Q. or by examination . . . are uneducational because they are based on an entirely obsolete view of growth".[2]

Such schools are experimenting in creating what might be termed a 'village school' atmosphere within the walls of the larger town school, aiming at reproducing the best that those versatile and flexible com-

---

[1] *The Plowden Report*: Volume 2, Appendix 11, Para. 2.3. shows that transfer between streams takes place far less often than it should.
[2] J. Blackie (formerly H.M. Chief Inspector for Primary Schools): *Inside the Primary School.*

munities have to offer. They have adopted some form of Vertical Classification—which merely means the more flexible grouping of various ages together in contrast to the horizontal, or traditional organization based on the 'standards', one (or more) for each year of the Junior school child's life, with automatic transfer to a higher class at the end of each academic year.

The most common form of Vertical Grouping (*not* vertical streaming) seems to be that spanning two year groups, i.e. 7+ to 9 years and 9+ to 11 years, but there is nothing arbitrary about this. A valuable aspect of Vertical Grouping is that, once the rigidity of the old one-year group and transfer is discarded, a variety of group combinations becomes possible. Thus possible variations are a 7+ to 9 years group, followed by 10-year and 11-year-old classes, or, should the numbers in the middle of the school be heavy, 7+ to 9 year classes, 9+ to 10 followed by an 11 year old class.

The system is flexible, and heads need no longer strain after producing as near as possible an approximation to the old one year-one class organization. Changes of class and teacher occur when most convenient: in practice this usually means approximately half a class of children, of mixed ability, moving on to a new class each year. The perplexities of deciding which children are suitable for which classes may not be eliminated but they are much reduced.

Why are Junior schools abandoning traditional organization for something akin to Infants' school Family Grouping?

A brief resumé of advantages and disadvantages follows, as outlined to the authors by heads and teachers themselves using the method.

Advantages

A more stable learning situation.

Opportunity for children to review and recapitulate their stages of progression.

Only half or less of the class changing each year, which lessens adjustment for children and teacher.

Advantages for the teacher include easier collaboration with each other (team teaching) and a longer period to get to know each child.

The children have a broader social experience with opportunity to lead, to follow, to collaborate, as well as to make stable peer relationships—very important in the latency period when peer groups are highly valued.

Elaboration on some of these points follows:

Learning

The learning situation remains stable for a longer period than the usual year.

Many young Junior children benefit from a longer association with a known adult than the yearly class organization allows. This is particularly important at the lower end of the school, where the concrete operational mode of thinking still dominates a child[1] and where there will normally be found a number of children still needing time and sound teaching to establish fluency in reading.[2] Stability and continuity of teaching are also particularly needed by the slow learner, by the unstable child or by the one with a broken or otherwise non-supporting home.

We now have a good understanding of the dependence of intellectual attainment upon suitable sequences of well-structured learning situations. We know that children's progress is not a steady climb upwards, but that he swings to and fro in his understanding, requiring opportunity to regress and to recapitulate in order that understanding may rest on a firm foundation. This is particularly so in the vital years of his concrete operational development, upon the success of which his ability to perform formal operations (to think and reason in the abstract) will depend.

A longer spell with the same teacher facilitates this progress which is sometimes imperceptible, without the anxiety and pressure of preparing for the next class up.

As for the teacher, where only half, or less, of the class changes each year, he has a longer period in which to get to know and understand his children. He is not faced with a large class of unknowns to whom he has to adapt each year. There is more protracted opportunity to watch over the children's intellectual development and to cater for it with appropriate material and teaching. In the words of one headmaster, "Stages, not ages, are what we look for".

At the same time, the fact that the children are securely based for a long period on the 'home' class, with the 'home teacher'[3] allows for other interesting developments in the school to take place.

Team Teaching

Vertical Classification is the ideal situation in which various forms of team teaching can take place.

Teachers and classes may be grouped in pairs, the strengths of one member of staff complementing those of the others. Probationers can pair with older, more experienced members: special talents in music, art and craft, science, mathematics or drama can be matched

---

[1] N. Isaacs: *The Growth of Understanding in the Young Child.*
[2] *The First Report of the National Development Study*, quoted in Appendix 10, Table 6 of the Plowden Report.
[3] Phraseology used in the Plowden Report.

and deployed without the swapping of whole classes, but simply by rearrangement of age groups within the two (or more).

Setting

Setting across year groups for special or graded teaching, say, in mathematics or French, is facilitated. Such internal rearrangements are doubly beneficial to the children, in that they have the security of a 'home' class and companions and a 'home' teacher whose pastoral care of them extends over two or even more years, whilst at the same time they benefit from contact with other teachers and from the diversity of talents on the staff. Teachers' own preferences can be exercised without their own classes becoming unduly disturbed.

Workshops

Workshop situations of various kinds are also developing in Junior schools.[1] Spare rooms or corridors are sometimes set up with a variety of equipment and apparatus in a particular field, for example, in mathematics, science, music and art/craft. The material is often used through assignments of tasks, which the children carry out in pairs or in groups. Another variation of 'workshop' practice is to allow the children a period of choice, varying from a whole morning or afternoon (variously known as 'workshop morning', 'club afternoon' or 'choice time'), to shorter times at the beginning or end of the day. All the resources of the classrooms, and the special interests of the staff are made available to the children according to their own preferences, sometimes with certain provisos, for example, that the chosen field of interest must be pursued for a reasonable length of time, say, for a month or a term.

The essence of these practices is that the children work in pairs or groups, and that they are no longer confined to the four walls of their classroom, the "traditional self-contained working base"[2]—and neither are the teachers. Teachers, as well as children, learn from one another, and a variety of opportunities is open to the children. But the stability of the school is not disrupted when the base classroom and teacher remain the same for such a long period.

Social Development

The young Junior child is entering a period when the personalities, skills and powers of his contemporaries are of growing significance to him. His trend will be increasingly away from dependence upon the adult and towards group interaction and membership. Satisfactory

---

[1] For some discussion of Mathematics workshops see *Mathematics in Primary Schools*, Curriculum Bulletin No. 1. H.M.S.O.
[2] Building Bulletin No. 36. *Eveline Lowe Primary School*, H.M.S.O.

exercise of this area of his personal life is of great importance. It has significant implications for his potential fulfilment.

There is reason to think that a mixed-age group gives better opportunity for the lively interplay and development of the various facets of social relationship. Over a long period there will be chances for a child to be subordinate and to follow, to play leadership roles, to control and to cooperate.

For cooperation there are striking opportunities. Class organization which does not rely upon disposition by examination automatically diminishes the feeling of competition, and this in turn provides opportunity to substitute cooperation between groups and individuals, and a policy of the improvement of personal standards rather than of beating one's neighbour. Competitive aggressiveness, which in the words of Dr. A. Storr[1] is "characteristic of immaturity", is an attribute which schools should surely seek to diminish rather than to foster.

"Instead of taking into account the child's deeper psychological tendencies which urge him to work with others, our schools condemn the pupil to work in isolation and only make use of emulation to set one individual against another", says Piaget,[2] writing of the traditional formal school. But schools which are less traditionally inclined have remarked upon the social and intellectual advantages which accrue from fostering cooperation, and in particular across age and ability groups. The headteacher of a village school of three classes, 5–7 years, 7–9 years and 9–11 years, speaking of children grouping themselves for topic work, says: "There is no question of the better ones looking down on the less able or younger, or the slow ones being overshadowed by the quick. They work together and help each other. Our job is to see that the children develop into human beings with an interest in, and compassion for each other, not only with concern for their own academic performance."

In reply to a question he went on, "No, the less able do not drag down the highflyers, rather the other way round."[3]

During most of the hours of traditional formal schooling a child is confined almost entirely to the dependent pupil/teacher role.

Save for a few, opportunities for leadership, cooperation and responsibility are minimal. But, teachers point out, in the less artificial atmosphere of a mixed age group more natural social conditions prevail. Since the mature man or woman is incomplete without satisfactory personal relationships it is desirable that these should develop

---

[1] A. Storr: *The Integrity of Personality.*
[2] J. Piaget: *The Moral Judgement of the Child.*
[3] It may be of interest to note that from this small village school each year some children move on without difficulty to high ranking independent schools. The staff provide "special textbooks for children with extra high I.Q.s". In other words no loss of standard is suffered by reason of the mixed age grouping.

174

appropriately from childhood, and that schools should facilitate this development. "The child from 8 to 11 or 12 still has to play out his social relationships," says E. B. Warr,[1] "and as he develops he demands a closer approach to reality." The mixed age group approximates more nearly to 'reality' than does the more contrived one of a narrow age group. In the wider social context of mixed ages, there is more chance for children's needs to complement one another, for them to give and take, drawing strength from and contributing to, their more natural miniature community.

A valuable intellectual advantage which accrues from the social mingling of wider age groups is the superior quality of discussion to which the younger ones are exposed, and in which they can participate. Most modern approaches to learning through firsthand experience emphasize the importance of the intelligent discussion of such experience for optimum benefit. Where the range of age and ability is wide, children obviously learn more from each other; vocabularies are extended, secondhand experiences broadened, more perceptive inferences drawn.

In the development of the idea of justice, discussion in mixed-age groups can be especially effective. In order to appreciate the notion of responsibility and self-discipline, the practice of considering underlying reasons for modes of behaviour should be cultivated. This is a sophisticated idea which children only master very gradually. A systematic policy of discussion rather than arbitary dispensation of justice by the adult helps to produce, by the age of 10 or 11 years, an appreciation of moral responsibility and respect for the framework of order necessary for society. Since the younger children are developing the tendency to admire and esteem their older contemporaries above the adult, their joint discussion of behaviour beneficial to the community at large minimizes disciplinary difficulties. Practical training in social responsibility is thus given, which might otherwise be left to too haphazard a chance. "The way in which he learns," says E. B. Warr, "should largely be the way of participation in group activity."

The sibling or kinship relationship which is preserved in most Family Grouped Infants' Classes may or may not be retained in the Junior School according to the discretion of the headteacher and staff. It will, in any case, begin to diminish in overt importance as it is supplemented by the growth of friendships.

The Junior child is normally in a period of temperamental stability which enables him to experiment with friendships without undue harassment to his feelings. But emotionally retarded or socially underdeveloped Juniors may find support and security in a further period of association with siblings, or perhaps make satisfying friendships with

---

[1] E. B. Warr: *Social Experience in the Junior School.*

those younger than themselves when they might otherwise remain solitary. The flexibility of Vertical Classification makes almost any beneficial combination of friends or family possible.

A further useful aspect of sound social training is that older children have the chance to give consideration to those younger or weaker than themselves.

Disadvantages

Most obvious are those associated with the intellectual development of and the teaching of a wide age and ability range.

A teacher relying too heavily upon traditional methods of class instruction will find the older and more able children quickly becoming under-extended and bored, whilst the younger ones may be over-shadowed and lose both heart and ground in their endeavours to keep up.

But given skilful use of modern active methods of learning and teaching, this wide range will be a source of strength, widening interests and adding to the resources of the class. The flexible organization calls for flexibility on the part of the teacher too. If the older and more able children are to be fully extended, so also will be the teacher. The challenge is to "translate into practice the principle of individual learning".[1]

Although this may seem at first a daunting prospect, it need not be so if it is appreciated that the learning achieved by individual children does not stem solely from the actual teaching of the teacher. The children learn from one another, from discussion, from books, from 'learning situations' planned by the teacher as well as from direct teacher teaching. Each child can contribute his individual interests, knowledge and ability, which, together with the children's not inconsiderable organizational capacity carries the class along with an impetus which cannot be achieved by a class teacher's drive alone.

But the task is a different one from that of the formal teacher, and mixed age groups are of small advantage if traditional methods are retained.

Other difficulties are those of providing a suitable range of books and equipment for each class, and of ensuring a varied programme of work over the longer period that a child spends with the same teacher. But these are administratively minor problems and are compensated for by the reduction of the annual upheaval of reforming all classes as in traditional organization.

There is no doubt that the main disadvantage could be that of the formal teaching method which depends too much upon class instruction and does not sufficiently involve the pupil in his own learning.

[1] *Children and their Primary Schools.*

For this reason a section follows which briefly reviews some of the ways of working which modern Junior schools are trying, and which are particularly suited to classes of mixed age and ability.

Ways of Working

Combined Subject Approach

Frequently termed 'topic work', this has become the established way of working in many primary schools. It is based on the pursuit of children's interests, and on the 'Discovery' approach, with children and teacher investigating together, and with the area of study broadening to embrace several of the disciplines formerly taught as separate units of the curriculum, such as history, geography, natural science, mathematics and so on. Linked and recorded by spoken and written language, which thus has partially displaced the formal 'English' of the old syllabuses, these studies have become so much a part of the Junior school curriculum that timetables are loosening up and Junior schools are well on the way to the 'integrated' or 'fluid' day which has made such strides in the Infant School world.

Such methods are ideally suited to the mixed age and ability class: each child can contribute according to his or her own ability, interest and experience, and will learn from the contributions of others.

Discussing the interdependence of adult members of the same society, Professor J. S. Bruner[1] points out that a culture is of it's very nature "a set of values, skills and ways of life that no one member of the society masters". He notes that in our educational system this "community of learning has been overlooked", and speaks of the need for individuals to cooperate together to "give support to learning by stimulating each person to join his efforts to a group". This is exactly what may be seen to be happening in classrooms where programmes of topic work are being followed.

Timetables become freer to allow adequate time to pursue group projects to a conclusion, and at the same time to give opportunity for the teacher to inject into the day such formal teaching as he thinks necessary.

Group Work and Creativity

Necessary formal teaching is usually given to children grouped together according to their capacities or levels of attainment, sometimes, as has been described, in a team teaching context.

There is no difficulty about combining such periods of instruction with a less formal approach. Children who are accustomed to working at their assigned or chosen aspects of group or class projects are

---

[1] J. S. Bruner: *Toward a Theory of Instruction.*

well able to use the time when the teacher's attention is given to others.

They also accept the pursuit of their own interests or work assignments as a proper part of school life, and many teachers have commented upon the fact that they will work purposefully and intelligently to improve their own standards and extend their knowledge.

A further development that fits well into the context of Vertical Classification is the freer approach to creative writing. Indeed, all aspects of creativity benefit from the elasticity of the flexible timetable component of the Vertically Classified classroom, as a child absorbed in a creative task can pursue it to its natural conclusion.

One headteacher of a very large Junior Mixed and Infants' School organized throughout on the 5–7, 7–9, 9–11 year basis, comments: "This is a very rewarding way of teaching and a self-perpetuating arrangement. The children, all but the newest entrants, have had experience of group and individual working, and are largely quite competent to organize themselves straight away."

Such a system harnesses the abilities of the children as well as those of the teacher, for the general good.

Extension of the Classroom

Classrooms are losing the formality of places where children merely follow instructions, and are becoming, in the words of Miss A. L. Murton, a former H.M.I., "a combination of workshop, studio and study".

Children overflow into corridors, library and other amenity areas, and there is more interplay of staff ability, especially when all combine in 'workshop' or 'free choice' time. Doors are more often open, and altogether buildings are being adapted to the more fluid nature of this kind of approach to primary school learning. The number and book 'corners' of the lower end of the primary school are being translated into bays, alcoves and resource areas, and special rooms are being set up, to form a "complex of work opportunities".[1] The children use these with poise and serious purpose because their learning experiences are suited to their own interests and their own levels of ability. "The dividing line between 'teaching' and 'non-teaching' becomes more indistinct as the whole building is drawn into use."[2]

Much work goes on in small groups, and schools are beginning to draw on auxiliary helpers and aides, and to enlist the supervisory help of parents, or to call upon their specialized knowledge.

For further discussion of these less traditional methods briefly referred to, but so necessary for the successful working of the mixed age and ability class, the reader is referred to the bibliography for

---

[1] Building Bulletin No. 36: *Eveline Lowe Primary School*.
[2] Ibid.

books on Junior school method, and in particular to the Plowden Report.

Records

We would like to state our opinion that an essential feature of the Vertically Classified class should be the systematic keeping of individual and group records. How else can the teacher be sure that in the diversity of activity and ability he has not lost sight of the progress of any one individual?

Class records need to contain a note of special interests pursued and topics followed, of poems, stories and songs, of areas of knowledge discussed. This ensures that repetition does not occur over a period of two years or so which might give rise to boredom, and also that important areas of learning are not neglected.

Individual records are essential, although they may take varied forms. Some teachers keep the traditional type, marking off in a record book certain prearranged milestones of progress, as in mathematics or reading. Others keep individual folders comprising samples of children's work collected every so often. A school is known to the authors where each child does a piece of work each month especially for his folder. Such a record, the contents of which will be known to each individual, has the merit of involving a child in his own standards of performance, and of encouraging him to make effort, not to beat others, but to improve upon his own previous achievement. The comparison standard then is not that of the competitive examination but of his own perfomances or in the words of one headmaster, "what the child did before".

Individual progress records will normally be supplemented by confidential comments on personality traits and family backgrounds, according to the practice of each school.

The keeping of such records, apart from being a serious professional obligation, provides useful information for teachers who will later handle the children, and the class records are valuable for supply teachers or those taking over at short notice.

Home—School Cooperation

In implementing a comparatively unfamiliar idea such as Vertical Classification, headteachers and staff may meet bewilderment, anxiety or even opposition on the part of parents, whose recollections of their own schooldays are often so very different.

In the interests of all, not least the children, full explanations should be given to parents both in advance of any major change and during the course of the terms to follow.

No novel method should ever be instituted without careful preparation, and this should always include an explanation to parents of the underlying philosophy of the school, the reasons for the particular change, and the expectations of the teachers in the long term results.

The gradual disappearance of the selective 11+ examination is opening the way for the Junior (Middle) schools to further experimentation into the best ways of educating their children. Changes in approach in method and in organization are afoot. But total rethinking may be necessary. Changes in organization cannot usefully be grafted onto methods and beliefs which are rooted in doctrinaire or authoritarian teaching and attitudes.

"A mere change in organization . . . unaccompanied by a serious attempt to change teacher's attitudes, beliefs and methods of teaching, is unlikely to make much difference either to attainment or . . . to the quality of teacher—pupil relationships" says the Plowden Report.[1]

Those who are curious about changes in traditional ways of teaching, or doubtful of their value may find useful the latest of Miss D. E. M. Gardner's[1] books on the subject, in the summary of which she says,

". . . to the many teachers who genuinely wonder whether the experimental methods may be advantageous or harmful to children, I hope this investigation may be helpful. . . ."

It is probably true to say that most changes occur because teachers become dissatisfied with already existing situations in the light of what they see happening to the children in them, and which, as knowledge and understanding of the nature of children and their learning processes grows, do not fit in with their changing beliefs about the best way to educate them.

One of the beliefs which is emerging from teacher's own experiences is that children may learn and develop better for not being regimented into the traditional homogeneous age or ability classes.

---

[1] *Children and their Primary Schools*, Volume 2, Appendix 11, Para. 3.4.
[1] D. E. M. Gardner: *Experiment and Tradition in Primary Schools*.

Bibliography

The authors are grateful to have been able to refer to the following publications:

Ainsworth, D.
An Aspect of the Growth of Religious Understanding of Children Aged 5–11 Years
(unpublished Dip. Ed. Dissertation, University of Manchester, 1961)

Allen, G. and others
Scientific Interests in the Primary School
National Froebel Foundation 1958

Bailey, Eunice
Discovering Music with Young Children
Methuen 1958

Bell, Vicars
On Learning the English Tongue
Faber and Faber 1953

Blackie, J.
Inside the Primary School
H.M.S.O. 1967

Bowley, A.
The Natural Development of the Child
E. and S. Livingstone 1957

Boyce, E.
The First Year in School
Nisbet 1953

Brearley, Molly
Studies in Education: First Years in School: The Practical Implications for the Teacher
Evans 1963

Brearley, Molly and Hitchfield, E.
A Teachers' Guide to Reading Piaget
Routledge and Kegan Paul 1966

Bruner, J. S.
Toward a Theory of Instruction
Harvard University Press 1966

Bühler, Charlotte
From Birth to Maturity
Routledge 1935

Cather, K.
Educating by Story Telling
Harrap 1919

Catty, N.
Learning and Teaching in the Junior School
Methuen 1956

Churchill, Eileen
Counting and Measuring in the Infants' School
Routledge 1961

Cooper, G.
The Place of Play in an Infants and Junior School
National Froebel Foundation 1963

Daniels and Diack
Progress in Reading
Educational Research, Vol. 6, No. 1 London 1963

Downing, J.
The Initial Teaching Alphabet
Cassell 1965

Downing, J.
Is a Mental Age of Six Essential for Reading Readiness?
Educational Research, Vol. 6, No. 1 London 1963

Gardner, D. E. M.
Long-Term Results of Infants' School Methods
Methuen 1950

Gardner, D. E. M.
Experiment and Tradition in the Primary School
Methuen 1956

Gesell, A. and Ilg, F.
The Child from Five to Ten
Hamish Hamilton 1950

Goddard, N.
Reading in the Modern Infants' School
University of London Press 1958

Goldman, R.
Studies in Education: First Years in School: Children's Spiritual Development
Evans 1963

Griffiths, R.
A Study of Imagination in Early Childhood
Kegan Paul 1935

Gutteridge, M.
Duration of Attention in Young Children
Melbourne University Press 1935

H.M.S.O.
Language: Some Suggestions for the Teacher of English and Others in Primary and Secondary Schools and in Further Education
1946

H.M.S.O.
Children and their Primary Schools
(The Plowden Report)
1967

H.M.S.O.
Mathematics in Primary Schools
(Curriculum Bulletin No. 1)
1965

H.M.S.O.
Eveline Low Primary School
(Building Bulletin No. 36)
1967

182

Hollamby, Lilian
Young Children Living and Learning
Longmans 1962

Hume, E.
Learning and Teaching in the Infants' School
Longmans 1948

Hughes, A. G.
Education and the Democratic Ideal
Longmans 1951

Isaacs, Nathan
Some Aspects of Piaget's Work
National Froebel Foundation 1956

Isaacs, Nathan
The Growth of Understanding in the Young Child
Ward Lock Educational 1961

Isaacs, Nathan
New Light on Children's Ideas of Number
Ward Lock Educational 1960

Isaacs, Susan
Intellectual Growth in Young Children
Routledge 1930

Jacks, M.
Total Education
Routledge 1947

James, H. and others
Periods of Stress in the Primary School
National Association for Mental Health 1956

Jordan, D.
Studies in Education: The Arts in Education: Movement and Dance
Evans 1963

Langdon, M.
Active Methods of Learning for Large Classes in the Junior School
National Froebel Foundation 1951

Langdon, M.
Let the Children Write
Langmans 1961

Lovell, K.
Educational Psychology and Children
University of London Press 1960

McFarland, H.
Psychology and Teaching
Harrap 1958

Mann, B.
Learning through Creative Work
National Froebel Foundation 1962

Marshall, Sybil
An Experiment in Education
Cambridge University Press 1963

Mellor, E.
Education through Experience in the Infants' School Years
Blackwell 1950

Melzi, K.
Art in the Primary School
Blackwell 1967

Nuffield Mathematics Teaching Project
Nuffield Foundation 1966

Nunn, P.
Education: Its Data and First Principles
Arnold 1945

National Union of Teachers
Report on Nursery-Infant Education
1949

Orff, Carl and Keetman G.
Music for Children
Schott 1961

Orton, S.
Reading, Writing and Speech Problems in Children
Chapman and Hall 1937

Peel, A.
The Psychological Basis of Education
Oliver and Boyd 1962

Piaget, J.
The Moral Judgement of the Child
Routledge and Kegan Paul 1932

Read, Herbert
Education through Art
Faber and Faber 1958

Reaney, M.
The Place of Play in Education
Methuen 1927

Reid, L. A.
Philosophy and Education
Heinemann 1962

Richmond, K.
Purpose in the Junior School
Alvin Redman 1949

Russell, Bertrand
Education and the Social Order
Allen and Unwin 1940

Sanderson, A.
A Re-Examination of the Idea of Reading Readiness
Educational Research, Vol. 6, No. 1 London 1953

Sealey, L. and Gibbon, V.
Communication and Learning in the Primary School
Blackwell 1964

Sealey, L. G. W.
The Creative Use of Mathematics in the Junior School
Blackwell 1961

Shedlock, M.
The Art of the Story Teller
Constable 1951

Simpson, D. and Alderson, D.
Creative Play in the Infants' School
Pitman 1960

Snydor, A.
Creating Music with Children
New York 1957

Stone, H.
Some Play Materials for Children Under Eight
National Froebel Foundation 1963

Storr, A.
The Integrity of Personality
Penguin 1963

Tanner, J. M.
Education and Physical Growth
University of London Press 1961

Terman, L. and Lims, M.
Children's Reading
Appleton 1931

Wall, W. D.
Education and Mental Health
H.M.S.O. 1955

Wall, W. D., Schonell, F. and Olson, W.
Failure in School
Hamburg 1962

Warr, E. B.
Social Experience in the Junior School
Methuen 1951

Watts, A.
The Language and Mental Development of a Child
Harrap 1944

Wheeler, D.
Studies in the Development of Reasoning in School Children
British Journal of Educational Psychology, Vol. 11 London 1958

Wheeler, O. and Earl, I.
Nursery School Education
University of London Press 1939

Whitehead, A.
The Adventure of Ideas
Cambridge University Press 1950

Yglesias, J. R. C.
Education for Living
Cory, Adams and Mackay 1965

Index

achievement 39, 75, 111
'activity' methods 26–34
adjusting 48–52
aggression 42, 49, 50
Ainsworth, D. 112
Alderson, D. 30, 49, 79, 110
Allen, G. 37, 109
anxiety 59–60
apparatus 36–38
Arts 41

Bailey, E. 120, 121, 123, 125
Bell, Vicars 103, 115, 118
Bowley, A. 42, 43–44, 46, 64
Boyce, E. 30, 35, 37, 82
Brearley, Molly 43, 78, 135
Bruner, J. S. 177
Bühler, Charlotte 66–67, 78
Burt 25

Cather, K. 116
'cell' classes 142–143
child psychology 42, 48–52
children, failing 59–60
    handicapped 56–58
children's personalities 20, 21–22,
    42–44
Churchill, E. 37, 86, 106, 109
Cizek 120
class lessons 112–129
classroom atmosphere 47–48
'conversation lesson' 80
Cooper, G. 27, 37
cooperation and competition 73–
    74
creative writing 98–103
Cuisenaire 108

Daniels, H. 85
Davies, Peter Maxwell 123
day-dreaming 48

development, emotional 40–63
    intellectual 75–111, 172, 175
    social 64–73
Dewey 23
Diack, D. 85
Dienes 108
disasters, fear of 50
discipline 22, 133, 175
disturbances, emotional 59–60
Downing, J. 84, 86
drama 118–120
drawing 81–82

Earl, I. 45
ego-involvement 28, 61, 62
equipment 36–38
    number 38
Erikson, E. 49, 50
experience, social 65–66, 173–176

failure 61
    fear of 50
Family Grouping 14–15
    arguments for 18–21
    arguments against 21–22
    changing over to 149–155
    children's views 166–168
    effects on children 158
    expense of 22
    parents' views 163–166
    teachers' views 156–163
    ways of using it 140–148
fantasy play 48–52
Free Day 30, 32–34, 45, 65
Froebel 23

Gesell, A. 25, 41, 42, 47, 48, 72,
    130, 132, 133
Gibbon, V. 30, 97–98, 109, 138–139
Goddard, N. 37, 90, 102
Goldman, R. 113, 114
grammar 101–103

Griffiths, D. 112
Griffiths, R. 24, 35, 43, 45–46, 49, 50, 51, 52, 53
growth, intellectual 75
growth, social 64–65
Gutteridge, M. 30

Hadfield, J. A. 51
handwriting 103–104
headteacher, role of 135–139
Hollamby, L. 30, 82, 89, 90, 116
Hughes, A 64, 78, 87, 131
Hughes, E. 131
Hume, E. 82, 116

Ilg, F. 41, 42, 47, 48, 72, 130, 132, 133
inferiority, feelings of 50, 66
integrated day, the 32–33, 177
insecurity 49
instruments, musical 123
Isaacs, Nathan 19, 25, 105, 108, 111
Isaacs, Susan 20, 24, 25, 26, 27, 33, 42, 46, 51, 59, 65, 79, 96, 110
ita 84, 87

Jacks, M. 41, 131
James, H. 53, 55, 74, 87, 133
Jordan, D. 118, 119

Klein 46, 51, 98

latency 48
learning, motivation for 24–26, 60–63
  success in 61–62
  failure in 62
  pleasure in 61
Lims, M. 116
literature 115–118
Lovell, K. 28, 48
Lowe Code 170
Lynn, R. 87

Mann, B. 37
Marshall, S. 91
mathematics 104–110, 173
maturation 25, 39, 42–44, 75, 111
McFarland, H. 48–49

Mellor, E. 23, 30, 82, 121
Montessori 23
music 120–127

number, understanding 104–111
Nunn, P. 23
'nurture' 39

Olson, W. 24, 39, 41, 60, 61, 75, 89
Orff, Carl 122
Orton, S. 81, 119

Paget, Sir Richard 119
Peel, A. 43
personality types 66–68
Pestalozzi 23, 81
Physical Education 41, 127–129
Piaget 19, 174
Plato 23
play 44–47
  creative 118–120
  dramatic 37
  fantasy 48–52
  groups 52–53, 72
  imaginative 118–120
'play way' 26–34
Plowden Report 169, 170, 172, 176, 180
poetry 115–118
'potency' 25
problem-solving 48–52
programmes, daily 29–34

Read, Herbert 126
reading 82–90, 96–98, 172
  readiness 84–88
Reavey, M. 62
records 133–135, 179
regression 17, 18, 52
Reid, L. A. 26, 36
relationships, child-teacher 132
  parent-teacher 132–133
Religious Education, 41, 112–115
responsibility 53, 65, 174
Richardson, Marion 120
Russell, Bertrand 16
Rousseau 23

Sanderson, A. 84, 85
Sayers 98

Schiller, L. C. 106
Schonell, F. 24, 39, 41, 60, 61, 75, 89
schools, British Forces 147–148
    nursery 146–147
    rural 143–146
school buildings 34–36, 178
school-home cooperation 20, 179–180
Sealey, L. 30, 97–98, 109, 138–139
selection, 11+170
Shedlock, M. 116
siblings 18, 40, 68–72
Simpson, D. 30, 49, 79, 90, 110
Snyder, A. 121
songs 121–122
spelling 101–103
'standards' 171
Stern 25
Stone, H. 46
stories 115–118
streaming 169
stress 54–55

talking 80–81
teachers, and Family Grouping 131–139
Teachers, National Union of 27, 35
team teaching 172–173

Terman, L. 116
'three Rs' 26, 27, 41, 43, 45, 75
timetables 30–34
topic work 177
Traditional Age-grouping 13–14, 16–17
Transitional Age - grouping 33, 140–142

Valentine 25
Vernon 25
Vertical Age-grouping 14–15
Vertical Classification 169–180
Viola, Dr. 120
vocabulary 80

Wall, W. 13, 15, 24, 38, 39, 40, 41, 42, 44, 56, 57, 59, 60, 61, 62, 75, 89, 111, 136
Watts, A. 80, 86, 118
Wheeler, D. 18–19
Wheeler, O. 45
Whitehead, A. 40
Williams, R. Vaughan 123–124
'workshop' classrooms 35–36, 173, 178
writing 53–54, 82–84, 89–103
    corner 38
    starting points 90–96